THE GREAT
HISPANIC HERITAGE

Simón Bolívar

THE GREAT HISPANIC HERITAGE

THE GREAT
HISPANIC HERITAGE

Simón Bolívar

Ronald A. Reis

CHELSEA HOUSE
P U B L I S H E R S
An imprint of Infobase Publishing

Chelsea House
An imprint of Infobase Publishing
132 West 31st Street
New York NY 10001

Library of Congress Cataloging-in-Publication Data
Reis, Ronald A.
  Simón Bolívar / Ronald A. Reis.
    p. cm. — (Great Hispanic heritage)
  Includes bibliographical references and index.
  ISBN 978-1-60413-731-6 (hardcover)
  1. Bolívar, Simón, 1783-1830—Juvenile literature. 2. Heads of state—South America—Biography—Juvenile literature. 3. South America—History—Wars of Independence, 1806-1830—Juvenile literature. I. Title. II. Series.
  F2235.3.R335 2010
  980'.02092—dc22
  [B]   2010009485

Chelsea House books are available at special discounts when purchased in bulk quantities for businesses, associations, institutions, or sales promotions. Please call our Special Sales Department in New York at (212) 967-8800 or (800) 322-8755.

You can find Chelsea House on the World Wide Web at http://www.chelseahouse.com.

Text design by Takeshi Takahashi
Cover design by Terry Mallon and Keith Trego
Composition by EJB Publishing Services
Cover printed by Bang Printing, Brainerd, MN
Book printed and bound by Bang Printing, Brainerd, MN
Date printed: September 2010
Printed in the United States of America

10 9 8 7 6 5 4 3 2 1

This book is printed on acid-free paper.

All links and Web addresses were checked and verified to be correct at the time of publication. Because of the dynamic nature of the Web, some addresses and links may have changed since publication and may no longer be valid.

Contents

The Making
of a Liberator

If the portrait of Simón Bolívar, painted on a porcelain miniature, is to be believed, the Caracas-born 22-year-old was, in 1805, as good-looking as he was vain. Bolívar's curly, almost kinky black hair complemented the dark and rough complexion of a fully shaven face. His eyes were frank and questioning, his nose long and handsome, his eyebrows thick and full, his cheeks decidedly prominent and sunken, his lips thick and, it was said, rather plain. Bolívar's teeth, which he studiously brushed many times a day, were white and radiant—and would remain so his entire life. The youthful, assertive, ever-animated Venezuelan creole, in Europe for an extended visit, stood but five foot six, on slim, rather bony legs, with a narrow, almost sunken chest.

Having, in recent months, exhausted his wild playboy persona, enjoying the pleasures of Paris, its gambling, women, and endless partying, Simón Bolívar now, in early August, found himself heading east with his tutor and mentor, Simón Rodríguez, for an extensive walking tour of Italy. How much the two actually hiked is unclear, but they did cross the Alps on foot, admiring both the romantic scenery and the Renaissance monuments along the way. In due course, the itinerant travelers entered Rome, where they were quick to take in much of what the historic "eternal city" had to offer.

Then, on August 15, Bolívar, with Rodríguez in tow, ascended the hill of Monte Sacro, where, according to legend, Sicinius led the people of Rome in protest against their patrician, or aristocratic, rulers. As the celebrated story goes, Bolívar became transfixed, his youthful immaturity giving way to a profound adult mission. According to Daniel O'Leary, a future friend and ardent supporter in all Bolívar would do, "On Monte Sacro the suffering of his own country overwhelmed his mind, and he knelt down and made that vow whose faithful fulfillment the emancipation of South America is the glorious witness."[1]

It is not known exactly what Simón Bolívar said that eventful day in Rome, as no one was taking notes. But according to Rodríguez, writing many years later, Bolívar fell to his knees, his eyes went wet, his breath heaved, and he cried out, "I swear before you, I swear by the God of my fathers, I swear by my fathers, I swear by my honor, I swear by my country that I will not rest body or soul until I have broken the chains with which Spanish power oppresses us."[2]

This vow, this oath Bolívar took on Monte Sacro, was by any standards a romantic, absurd conceit, made by an idealistic, still petulant and unaccomplished snob. Yet a mere 20 years later, Simón Bolívar would claim to rule one of the greatest empires in history, covering 3 million square miles (7.7 million square kilometers) in South America, more than eastern and western Europe combined. To do it, and to free six Latin American countries from 300 years of Spanish colonial domination, Bolívar would travel 20,000 miles (3,218 km) on horseback and fight almost 300 battles and skirmishes unscathed. For millions—white, brown, and black people

Despite the fact that Simón Bolívar was born into privilege and given many opportunities, the Spanish considered him inferior due to his creole background. Bolívar, who was smart and eager to prove himself, seized his chance for leadership when the Spanish Empire in Caracas began to crumble.

alike—Simón Bolívar would become their "Liberator," their freedom-fighter extraordinaire.

SPOILED CREOLE

Simón Bolívar was born into a rich, landowning creole family on July 24, 1783, in Caracas, the capital of the Spanish colonial possession of Venezuela. His mother died when Simón was three; his father when he was nine. As an infant, Bolívar was, for the most part, raised apart from his parents, in particular by a nurse named Hipólita, a black slave.

The hyperactive Simón grew up spoiled, impulsive, and bossy, accustomed to getting his own way at nearly every turn. It wasn't long before extended family members grew frustrated with the task of raising Simón, and he was quickly sent off to be educated by a succession of tough-minded tutors. "Each in turn despaired, finding him one of the most unpleasant small boys they had ever dealt with—boastful, imperious, irrepressible, demanding, and fiercely insolent,"[3] declared historian Robert Harvey. In 1795, at the age of 12, Bolívar was sent to the home of Simón Rodríguez, a tutor who would have a profound influence on the future Liberator's thinking and actions.

On January 18, 1799, Simón Bolívar, not yet 16, was sent off to Madrid, Spain, where it was hoped his cockiness and arrogance would be lessened by exposure to European culture and Spanish adult supervision. Rather than being impressed with any elevated standards of Spanish conduct, however, Simón, having been presented to members of the royal court, soon found himself squirming amid unattractive and over-indulging elders. Bolívar would take from the experience a profound contempt for the empire they represented.

In early 1802, Simón was introduced to a young woman two years his senior, María Teresa Rodríguez del Toro. He found her irresistibly beautiful, gentle, and almost childlike in her purity. Against both families' wishes, the two married the following May. Simón was not yet 19.

The couple sailed at once for Caracas and upon arrival made their home in the heart of the city. Almost immediately, tragedy struck the young honeymooners. María Teresa contracted a fever and died on January 22, 1803. Simón, half-mad with grief, vowed never to marry again.

In part to lessen his profound distress, Bolívar again took off for Europe, this time choosing to settle in Paris. Here he drowned himself in reckless gambling and sensual pleasures. According to Serviez, one of Bolívar's aides, "It was truly exciting to hear The Liberator name all the beautiful girls he had known in France, with a precise recollection that does honor to his powers of memory."[4]

It wasn't all frenzied affairs for Simón, however. On December 2, 1804, Bolívar found himself in an overflowing crowd in front of Notre Dame, there to witness the crowning of Napoléon I (Napoléon Bonaparte) as emperor of France. "That which seemed great to me was the universal acclaim and the interest which the person of Napoleon inspired," the youth later recalled. "I confess this made me think of my country's enslavement, and of the glory that would cover the man who liberated her."[5] Seven months later, South America's future emancipator would climb Monte Sacro in Rome.

SPANISH AMERICA

Every American knows the significance of "1492," the year Christopher Columbus set foot in the New World. Less well known, however, is the fact that in the same year, Spain, after a five-century struggle, achieved the *Reconquista* ("Reconquest") of its lands by finally banishing Muslims from the Catholic Iberian Peninsula. In the half millennium it took to accomplish this objective, a Hispanic way of life materialized around titled fighting men. It was these warring individuals, the conquistadores, following in the wake of Columbus, who would set the stage for Spanish rule and misrule in the New World.

In time, the conquistadores were joined by a growing number of merchants, lawyers, clergy, and royal officials, the vast majority of whom looked down, with utter contempt, on individuals engaged in any type of manual labor. It would be these royal officials, through the governing entities of viceroyalties and captaincy generals, that would exploit

and brutalize the Native Indians and African slaves—the former in working the gold and silver mines of, in particular, Mexico and Peru, and the latter, on vast sugar and cotton plantations on the continent and also in the Caribbean Islands.

Significantly, few women came from Spain to the Americas, particularly in the first century after the conquest. As a result, a great deal of racial mixing took place among Europeans, Native Indians, and Africans. The offspring of Europeans and Indians were called mestizos. The children of Europeans and Africans were mulattoes. And those of Indians and Africans were known as *zambos* (the origin of the word *sambo* in English). Within a short time, a clear social pyramid developed, with creoles (whites born in the Americas) at the top, followed by mestizos, mulattoes, and zambos. Native Indians were only slightly elevated from the lowest in the human pecking order—African slaves.

To be sure, creoles weren't actually at the societal apex. Significantly above them were the rulers of Spain's vast possessions in the New World: the royal officials, who were part of the larger peninsular class, made up of whites born in the mother country. Such *peninsulares*, racist to the core, would soon come to look down on their creole "brothers," who in their eyes had begun to absorb too many native traits, and thus were seen as exotic and crude compared to their compatriots from Madrid. As the centuries wore on, the antagonisms that developed between these two groups, peninsular Spaniards and creoles, would lead to the long and bloody fight for Latin American independence.

CREOLE DISCONTENT

There can be little doubt that peninsular Spaniards held a privileged status in late-eighteenth-century Latin America. Of the 170 viceroys who governed in America until 1813, only four were creoles. Of the 602 captains general and presidents, only 14 were born in the colonies.[6] Referring to New Spain (Mexico), but applicable throughout Spanish America, historian Lucas Alamán noted, "They [peninsular Spaniards]

FERDINAND VII OF SPAIN

Ferdinand VII, known as Ferdinand the Desired, was born on October 14, 1784, and died on September 29, 1833. He was king of Spain twice, in 1808 and again from 1813 to 1833. With the French invasion of Spain in 1808, Napoléon I abducted Ferdinand and took him back to France, where he remained under guard for six years at the Chateau de Valençay. Technically, Ferdinand had abdicated his throne, with Napoléon placing his brother, Joseph Bonaparte, in his place. Some in the Spanish government accepted Ferdinand's abdication, but many Spaniards did not. Uprisings broke out throughout the country, resulting in what became known as the Peninsular War.

With Napoléon's defeat looming in late 1813, Ferdinand VII was returned as king of Spain. But the country Ferdinand had left six years earlier was no longer the same. A liberal constitution had been passed in 1812, and Ferdinand was expected to rule under it. He did not, and sought to establish an absolute monarchy once more.

Ferdinand VII was married no less than four times, twice to nieces. The last niece bore him two daughters. Ferdinand died a bloated, apathetic, and, it was said, difficult-to-look-at man. With him passed the concept of the divine right of kings, where it was assumed that a king must be wiser than his ministers since he was placed on the throne by God. Ferdinand had clearly failed to justify the argument.

occupied nearly all the principal posts in the administration, the church, the judiciary, and the army; commerce was almost exclusively in their hands; and they possessed large fortunes, consisting of cash, which they employed in various lines of business and in all kinds of farms and properties."[7] Given the peninsular Spaniards' privileged position, as compared to the creoles, Alamán pointed out, "It is not difficult to explain the jealousy and rivalry that steadily grew between them, resulting in a mortal enmity and hatred."[8]

Spain's colonial system was designed to take all it could through mining and agriculture for the Spanish market. It was into this quintessential plantation society that Simón Bolívar was born. As an adult, he soon enough saw clearly its exploitive nature. "The Americans, in the Spanish system now in place, perhaps more so than ever before, have no other place in society than that of simple consumers," the future liberator would write. "Even in this they are burdened with shocking restrictions, such as a ban on the cultivation of European fruit . . . a prohibition on factories which not even the peninsula possesses, exclusive commercial privileges even over basic needs, and customs bans between American provinces so that they cannot trade, understand each other, or negotiate."[9]

Through such economic polices, Spain (as the centuries wore on) became ever more backward and parasitic. "Blessed" with a continuous influx of precious metals and agricultural goods, the mother country, unlike many of its European neighbors, failed to develop a significant industrial and commercial base. As a result, "By the late eighteenth century, the colonies were groaning under the impact of low prices, high taxation, and the prohibition of trade with countries other than Spain."[10]

Yet even with all the burdens imposed on the creole class by Spanish rulers, the former failed to rise up in protest because they feared any action would unleash similar revolts by those below them: the masses of "colored" discontents,

Following Christopher Columbus's discovery of the New World in 1492, an influx of European explorers and settlers rushed into North America. Spanish warriors, or conquistadores (*above*), were sent overseas on behalf of the Spanish Empire and established settlements throughout the Caribbean, Central America, and South America.

particularly the blacks. In 1804, just such a "calamity" took place on the island of Hispaniola, in Haiti. Black slaves broke free and took control, killing hundreds of white administrators and landowners in the process. Such social violence from the disenfranchised blacks frightened creoles into the shelter of the colonial state. If, however, the mother country itself were to falter, if Spain were to crumble, what would the creoles do? Would they be forced to seek their own security, in a complete break from the empire that had ruled them for 300 years?

THE FRENCH SPARK

A number of key factors, or forces, would now, in the first decades of the nineteenth century, combine to plunge Latin America into its wars for independence.

Creole discontent was key. The economic and political restriction they experienced at the hands of peninsular Spaniards irked and grated on the proud white Americans.

French and English liberal thought, pronounced by such writers as Jean-Jacques Rousseau and Charles-Louis de Secondat, baron de La Brède et de Montesquieu, emphasized the rights of man and the limits of monarchy, and so influenced the learned creole class. So, too, did the examples of the American and French revolutions.

Furthermore, foreign powers, particularly England, wanted to see Spain's Latin American empire implode so they could benefit from open and liberal trade.

These factors aside, the spark, the tipping point that actually set the Spanish-American revolutions in motion came from one decisive event—the invasion of Spain by French troops in 1808. In the process, Spain's King Ferdinand VII was taken prisoner and brought to France. In consequence, the Spanish people rose up and established juntas, or local governing committees, to rule in the king's absence.

Creole leaders in the Spanish colonies, taking advantage of Spain's distress, also established juntas, while at the same time professing loyalty to "the beloved Ferdinand VII." On April 19,

1810, Venezuela led the way, and in a bloodless revolt deposed the Spanish captain general. The "revolution" had begun.

While the newly established Caracas junta represented the creole ruling class, it did not speak with one voice. As John Lynch was quick to note, "It [the junta] was divided between conservatives who saw themselves as holding the fort for a captive king and the traditional order, autonomists who wanted home rule within the Spanish monarchy, and supporters of independence who demanded an absolute break with Spain."[11] To which faction Simón Bolívar belonged, there could be little doubt. "Not for him adhesion to an absent king and spurious institutions in Spain, or to those in Venezuela who took these things seriously," declared John Lynch. "Full independence was the only serious choice."[12]

In an attempt to seek support for its actions, the Caracas junta early on decided to send a delegation to London. Two experienced, mature adults, Luis López Méndez and Andrés Bello, were quickly chosen as emissaries. Bolívar begged to be included. Junta leaders were reluctant to accept the young, reckless, and extravagant patriot, but when he offered to pay the costs for the entire delegation, they acquiesced and appointed him nominal leader. On July 10, 1810, the three-man Venezuelan mission arrived in Portsmouth, England. From there they traveled to London, hoping to be received by the British Foreign Office.

Lord Arthur Wellesley, the British Foreign Secretary, did receive Bolívar's delegation, but not officially, for England had no intention of recognizing the fledging republic. To do so would alienate Spain, essentially at war with Britain's archenemy, France. Though there would be few tangible diplomatic results from the mission, the envoys did gain international attention for the Venezuelan cause, itself in the vanguard of junta movements springing up throughout Spanish America. Simón Bolívar, still ever full of himself despite proving to be a rather naïve diplomat, would return to Venezuela a "leader in waiting."

Miranda
and Bolívar

Francisco de Miranda, born in 1750 of wealthy creole parents in Caracas, Venezuela, grew up every bit as privileged, spoiled, and downright insufferable as Simón Bolívar. As a child, he was frequently found playing with neighborhood children, sipping cold drinks on hot days and munching on perfumed chocolates. In 1771, at the age of 21, Miranda took a two-month journey across the Atlantic to Cádiz, Spain. In December of the following year, he joined the Spanish army as an infantry captain. "He cut a strong and unusual figure, tall and well-built, always immaculately and expensively dressed. . . . His chin jutted confidently, and his hair fell forward insouciantly [lightheartedly] over a large brow. His looks made him irresistible to women, and as vain as a peacock."[1]

A decade later, Miranda, though having proven himself an able and prominent officer, had nonetheless grown tired of the ever-present arrogance his Spanish overlords continued to display toward him, a mere creole. Having, on an earlier occasion, visited the United States (where he met Alexander Hamilton, Thomas Paine, and George Washington—all leaders of American independence), Miranda concluded that liberation of the Spanish colonies was soon to follow. In 1785, the man who would become known as El Precursor ("The Forerunner") set up headquarters in London. The time was ripe, he concluded, for public advocacy of Latin American freedom.

It would be another 25 years, however, before Miranda, through the vehicle of Simón Bolívar, would take the lead in fighting to free Venezuela from Spanish control. In July 1810, the two, separated by 33 years in age, met for the first time in London. His recent diplomatic mission less than a success, Bolívar nonetheless did succeed in persuading Miranda to return to Venezuela and lead the battle for independence. On December 11, 1810, a few days behind Bolívar, the 60-year-old Miranda arrived in Caracas to a tumultuous welcome.

As Miranda settled in, it became clear that his reception by the creole elite would be decidedly mixed. He fully believed he had returned to his homeland, destined to be its liberator. His lifelong conceit quickly surfaced, however. "At the banquets which were held for him, he received the toasts in his honour without a word of reply, without raising his glass, simply smiling benevolently, like a king with his subjects."[2]

Many of the creole leadership viewed Miranda as a foreigner and as an old man out of touch with what was happening in Venezuela. Indeed, the moderate Caracas junta formed in April had initially planned to bar El Precursor from entering the country. It was only through Bolívar's intervention, on behalf of a man he idolized, that Miranda was allowed to set foot on Venezuelan soil.

DECLARATION OF INDEPENDENCE
Divisions within the Caracas junta aside, in February 1811 Miranda was appointed a lieutenant general by the country's

After the death of his wife, Bolívar spent some time in Europe before returning home and joining the cause for his country's liberation. He joined Caracas's Patriotic Society and quickly became one of their most prominent members. *Above*, the Venezuelan Congress declares their country's independence on July 5, 1811.

new Congress. Bolívar, meanwhile, became active in Caracas's Patriotic Society, a group of elite creoles meeting to discuss questions of economics and good government. The Congress and the Patriotic Society were often at odds. On July 3, Bolívar, addressing the Congress in a night session, made his first significant political speech when he declared, "The Patriotic Society respects, as it must, the nation's Congress; but Congress must listen to the Patriotic Society, centre of light and of all revolutionary interests. Let us lay down the cornerstones of South American freedom. To vacillate is to yield!"[3]

There was no turning back now. Though creole leaders had often expressed support throughout the past year for Spain's Ferdinand VII, in truth such an allegiance was a mere facade, known as "the mask of Fernando," whereby a junta could claim fidelity to a leader who was in no position to lead. On July 5, 1811, Congress declared Venezuela an independent republic. It was the first clear declaration of independence anywhere in South America.

To announce independence was one thing, to obtain and keep it, however, was quite another. Divisions within the movement cause soon surfaced. For starters, two distinct factions emerged. One, which both Miranda and Bolívar strongly favored, sought a unitary government, with a strong Caracas-based centralized state. The other, however, favored a federal, decentralized form of government, where scattered cities and rural communities throughout Venezuela would be given a great deal of autonomy. In December 1811, in a significant defeat for Miranda and Bolívar, a new written constitution granted internal self-government to each major city. Thus Venezuela's First Republic would be a federal republic, with the provinces given ample power to deal with local affairs and the central authorities in Caracas in charge of more general interests.

Bolívar was not happy with the structure of Venezuela's new government. Clearly, having been influenced by the U.S. federal model, Bolívar firmly believed that "the choice of federalism reflected an unwholesome fascination with foreign models that were inapplicable to Venezuela."[4] In particular, Bolívar was gravely concerned that federalism was inappropriate for such a fledging government. What such a government needed, he felt, was a highly centralized regime, one with strong executive power.

As Caracas asserted its independence from Spain, the provinces began to claim rights from Caracas. Since the constitution granted suffrage only to those who owned property (creole elite) and denied it to those who didn't (for the most part, *pardos*, nonwhites), urban-rural tensions soon manifested. With the white overclass outnumbered by Indians, free blacks, and slaves (by four-to-one), the former were clearly nervous. Independence aside, the creole urban elite and large landowners were quick to set limits of freedom and equality for the lower classes. Not a good omen for a united fight against a mother country determined to retain its colonial power.

COUNTERREVOLUTION

That Spain would be quick to contest any rebellion soon became apparent just three weeks after independence was declared, when fighting broke out in the city of Valencia, approximately 80 miles (128.7 km) west of Caracas. Desperate royalists in the city, with the aid of armed *pardos*, declared themselves for Ferdinand VII. A patriot force sent out from Caracas to subdue the counterrevolutionaries was defeated. In a panic, the Venezuelan Congress nominated Miranda generalissimo (the only experienced independence-support-ing general). His immediate mission was to take Venezuela's second-largest city.

On July 23, Miranda moved his army of 4,000 peasants, "poorly trained, badly armed and all marching out of step," toward Valencia. "He disdainfully asked his aides where were the armies which a general of his prestige 'could bring to the battle without compromising [his] dignity.'"[5]

It is at this time, on the eve of a potentially decisive battle in the struggle for independence, that Miranda, for no apparent reason except to feed his vanity, turned on Bolívar, his protégé, and denounced him as a dangerous and uncon-trollable young man. Bolívar, having hoped to serve directly under Miranda, was stunned. Nursing the offense, Bolívar nevertheless secured a post under Francisco Jose Rodriguez del Toro e Ibarra, cuarto marqués del Toro, Miranda's sec-ond in command.

Upon reaching the hills of El Morro on the outskirts of Valencia, patriot forces were suddenly ambushed. Though the attacking forces fell back in confusion, Bolívar, yelling and wav-ing his sword, spurred them onward, "displaying both bravery and ferocity in this, his first engagement."[6] Nonetheless, the patriot army was forced to retreat. Over 800 attacking soldiers were killed; close to twice that many were wounded.

Miranda now laid siege to Valencia. He stopped food, water, and supplies from entering the city. Finally, on August 13, royalists, facing possible starvation, surrendered. Miranda's forces entered the city in triumph and promptly sacked it. The patriots, if only because of superior numbers, had won the first major campaign of the Latin American wars of independence.

Yet the boastful, arrogant, and jealous Miranda could not, even after praising Bolívar in a written report as having fought with distinction, refrain from publicly humiliating his disciple. In a parade after the battle, Miranda berated Bolívar for indiscipline. It was clear that, although their cause was the same, the

SPANISH RULING STRUCTURE

At the dawn of the nineteenth century, Spanish rule in Latin America took place through its four viceroyalties (vice-kingdoms), structured as follows:

Viceroyalty of New Spain (established in 1535) This viceroyalty embraced the Audiencia of Mexico and the Audiencia of Santo Domingo, as well as the Captaincy General of Guatemala and Cuba.

Viceroyalty of New Granada (established in 1739) This viceroyalty included the presidency of Quito (Ecuador), the Audiencia of Santa Fé de Bogotá, and the Captaincy General Audiencia of Caracas.

Viceroyalty of Peru (established in 1543) This, the most powerful and richest of Spanish viceroyalties, embraced the Audiencia of Cuzco and the Captaincy General of Santiago de Chile.

Viceroyalty of La Plata (established in 1776) This viceroyalty was subdivided into the Audiencia of Buenos Aires, the presidency of Asunción (Paraguay), the presidency of Charcas (Bolivia), and the Banda Oriental (Uruguay).

older revolutionary would not suffer the upstart younger one. Bolívar endured the slight in silence, though the wound would fester for a lifetime.

Miranda, demonstrating his cautious approach to warring, refrained from following up on the Valencia victory by withholding support for embattled patriots in nearby towns such as Coro, Maracaibo, and Guayana. Miranda, a man of strictly European military training, would argue that he needed more time to prepare the patriot forces, that they required further rigorous training before committing themselves anew.

As the year 1812 dawned, the new country of Venezuela, though free in name and in places, faced formidable obstacles to obtaining lasting independence from the rule of Spain. Under a Spanish blockade, Venezuela's economy lay in ruins, with vast lands going uncultivated and trade at a near standstill. The government, no longer in control of a large part of the country, fell into factional dispute. The war for true independence was anything but won.

DIVINE RETRIBUTION

On March 26, 1812, two years to the day after the Caracas City Council deposed the Spanish viceroy, a severe earthquake struck northeastern Venezuela, shaking violently from the Andes to the coast. As church bells throughout the land rang out in frantic, tumbling discord, thousands of early Easter worshippers perished among the ruins of collapsing buildings, particularly houses of worship. On this Holy Thursday, the church of San Jacinto, in Caracas, completely tumbled to its foundation, killing dozens of men, women, and children. "As cries for help were heard from the ruins, mothers were seen bearing children in their arms desperately trying to revive them, and desolate families wandered in a daze through clouds of dust seeking missing fathers, husbands, and friends."[7] In dozens of patriot-held towns and cities, wreckage was everywhere. The great army barracks at San Carlos plunged down upon a regiment waiting to march.

Francisco de Miranda, a Venezuelan military hero, fought in the Spanish
military and was involved in both the American and French revolutions.
Bolívar managed to persuade Miranda to return to their homeland and lead
the people to independence, but the general's arrogance and vanity soon
had the two leaders at odds.

On April 4, a second earthquake struck, raising the death toll in Caracas to over 20,000.

Bolívar, slumbering on the oppressively hot Caracas day in March, was instantly shaken awake. "I immediately set about trying to save the victims, kneeling and working towards those places where groans and cries of help were coming from," he was to declare later. "I was engaged upon this task when I saw the pro-Spanish José Domingo Diaz, who looked at me and commented with his usual scorn: 'How goes it, Bolívar? It seems that nature has put itself on the side of the Spaniards.' 'If nature is against us, we will fight it and make it obey us,' I replied furiously."[8]

Indeed, it would not be long before priests throughout Venezuela would claim to have seen God's wrath in the earthquake that had destroyed nine-tenths of Caracas and killed thousands. Royalist strongholds, such as Valencia, Coro, Maracaibo, and Guayana, as well as large segments of the royalist army, were unaffected. Many priests asserted this was divine retribution; punishment from on high for those who had rejected the Lord's anointed King Ferdinand VII. Survivors hurried to renew their vows to both God and Spain. The morale of patriot forces plummeted. Ordinary Venezuelans by the thousands, now swung over to the royalist cause.

From this destruction, there arose a new royalist commander: Domingo Monteverde, a former Spanish naval captain, with a decidedly vengeful and cruel disposition. As he moved his forces forward and outward, patriot towns were butchered and sacked. "Neither women nor children could find mercy."[9]

In response to a desperate situation, Congress granted Miranda dictatorial powers. At the age of 62, the aging generalissimo was seen as the patriots' only hope. Yet, the graying leader was not optimistic. "They have approached me to preside over Venezuela's funeral," Miranda was to have declared, "but I cannot deny my services to my country in the calamitous circumstances in which man and nature have placed it."[10]

BETRAYAL

In part because of the bravery he had shown at El Morro, Miranda sent Bolívar, now a colonel, to command the garrison town of Puerto Cabello, a strategic gateway to the sea for Caracas. It was here that a large number of royalist prisoners were kept at the main fort, as well as a huge stockpile of arms and artillery. On June 30, while Bolívar amused himself playing cards, a group of prisoners seized control of the castle fortress. Royalists could now fire down upon Bolívar's forces. Bolívar sent an urgent message to Miranda, imploring him to provide assistance. The letter did not arrive in time, however. A few days later, Bolívar and a number of officers managed to escape in a small boat. In his first command and only second engagement, 22-year-old Simón Bolívar failed miserably. He dragged himself off to Caracas, locked himself in his house, and refused to see anyone, dejected beyond consoling.

In his depressed (some would say psychotic) state, Bolívar now penned the first of two infamous letters to Miranda. "My general: After having exhausted all my material and spiritual resources, only with whatever courage remains could I dare to take up the pen to write to you, having lost Puerto Cabello at my own hands. . . . I did my duty, my general, and if the soldiers had remained on my side, I would have had enough strength to fight the enemy. If they abandoned me, it was not my fault. Nothing remained for me to do to contain the enemy and . . . save the fatherland. But, alas! This was lost in my hands."[11]

This first hysterical, shrill, and whining letter was soon followed by an even more groveling, imploring one. "My general, my head, my heart, they are good for nothing. I beg you to permit me an interval of a few days to see if my mind can be returned to its ordinary state. After having lost the best fortress in the land, how can I not be insane, my general? Please do not oblige me to see you face to face. I am not to blame, but I am dispirited and it is enough."[12]

Summing up Bolívar's reaction to his first major military calamity, historian Robert Harvey observed, "Bolívar did not yet possess the inner force which alone could hold together his many and discordant parts. His youthful petulance and vanity were not of the fiber which his unruly self needed. They had first to be crushed by the hammer of adversity."[13]

With the patriot's situation now all but lost, Miranda, on July 25, sued for peace. Insurrections broke out all over. It was every man for himself. As Miranda prepared to escape by ship, Bolívar and several officers met secretly to denounce the general's "betrayal." They argued that Miranda must be turned over to Spanish authorities. Bolívar went so far as to demand that Miranda, his heretofore idol, be summarily shot. Hoping to ingratiate themselves to the Spanish by handing over the Precursor, the band of patriot officers did just that. Miranda would die in a Cádiz prison four years hence. It was anything but Bolívar's finest hour. Any "betrayal," it seemed to some, was not Miranda's alone.

3

War to
the Death

Bolívar's defeat and disgrace at Puerto Cabello had a transforming effect on the young patriot. Finally rising from his stupor and self-pity, he made it to the sunbaked tropical island of Curaçao, 50 miles (80.4 km) off the Venezuelan coast, where he was destined to spend poverty-stricken weeks in late August and September 1812. It was here the once easygoing Bolívar morphed into a passionate, ruthless avenger. "By the same methods as the oppressors of Caracas managed to subdue the confederation, with those same methods and with more certainty than them, I will try to redeem my fatherland,"[1] he wrote. Bolívar would now attempt to do so, with both the sword and the pen.

In October, Bolívar sailed to the Caribbean port of Cartagena, New Granada, with its impenetrable fort. Two years earlier, the city had risen up, claiming its right to free trade. In Bogotá, the New Granadian capital 400 miles (643.7 km) to the south, the viceroy was arrested. Then, in an attempt at self-rule, Cartagena declared itself a city-state, refusing to submit to Bogotá's dominance. By 1812, while New Granada was claiming its independence from Spain, it became engulfed in civil war. According to John Leach, "The Spaniards simply had to wait for New Granadians to destroy each other."[2]

Upon Bolívar's arrival in Cartagena, the patriot governor, Manuel Rodríguez Torices, desperate for fighting men, appointed him a colonel. Soon after, a rival of Torices's, General Labatut, sent Bolívar literally down the Magdalena River to the small, isolated town of Barrancas. It is here that Bolívar settled in to compose the Cartagena Manifesto—perhaps his most famous pronouncement on the South American wars for independence.

To Bolívar, it was internal dissension, not Spanish arms, that had defeated the First Republic in Venezuela. "The most far-reaching error Venezuela committed when it entered politics was without any doubt the disastrous adherence to a system of tolerance; a system proved by the whole thinking world to be weak and ineffective, yet tenaciously adhered to with exceptional blindness to the very end," he wrote on December 15, 1812. Bolívar then went on to declare, "Federalism, though it may be the most perfect [system] and the most capable of bringing happiness to human society, is nevertheless the most detrimental to the interests of our infant countries. Generally speaking our citizens are not yet able to exercise their rights fully and for themselves, because they lack the political virtues that characterize true republics."[3]

In sum, Bolívar made it clear that while he was a republican at heart, for South Americans to win their independence, they would have to be disciplined, united, professionally trained, and, when necessary, just as ruthless as the enemy they faced. Bolívar was determined to try again. This time, though, the would-be Liberator proposed to launch an expedition from the Andean Territory where he now resided. Bolívar would seek to free both New Granada and Venezuela (along with Ecuador), and in so doing form what he would eventually call "Gran Colombia."

"ADMIRABLE CAMPAIGN"

Bolívar disobeyed orders to stay put in Barrancas, to be in a strictly defensive position. Remaining passive was not his style. In late December 1813, he oversaw the construction of a flotilla of canoes and rafts and headed up the Magdalena River. Initiating a surprise attack, he and his band of 200 volunteers seized the town of Tenerife from a royalist detachment. With the acquisition of abandoned arms, Bolívar then advanced upstream, taking one Spanish position after another. Within two weeks, the 30-year-old commander had broken the royalist blockade of the Magdalena River. The government of Cartagena, its morale instantly elevated, happily overlooked Bolívar's insubordination and urged him on, out of the Magdalena Valley to Ocaña, a small city on the eastern side of the Andes.

Hearing of the now famous warrior's approach, the Spanish garrison at Ocaña quickly fled. Bolívar entered the city in triumph. The whole province of Cartagena was suddenly free of Spanish control. Gratifying as his recent victories were, Bolívar's real objective, however, lay in eventually recapturing Caracas. To that end, he now advanced to the town of Cúcuta, on the border between New Granada and Venezuela. Though outnumbered 500 to 800, Bolívar, leading a furious bayonet charge, quickly captured the royalist stronghold. It was by all accounts a major victory.

In just two months, Bolívar had succeeded in seizing numerous enemy strongholds, one after the other. He had initiated a form of attack based, not on a European model, but on the topography and conditions he encountered. "His forces had proved themselves masters of a new type of warfare," wrote Robert Harvey, ". . . guerrilla attack, the movement of relatively small armies across large distances

Defying congressional orders, Bolívar left his defensive post in Granada and proved that he was a capable, effective military leader. He was given approval to march on Venezuela, where he incorporated the information on local topography and geography to fight his battles, revolutionizing the country and the art of war.

to inflict surprise attacks on sleepy outposts where they were least expected. . . . His crossing of the cordillera [mountain] was a deed of astonishing speed and endurance, the first of a series of near-superhuman feats of generalship and leadership carried out over some of the most geographically varied, taxing and savage terrain on earth. He had turned the terrible topography to his advantage."[4]

Successful as he now was, Bolívar hungered to move forward, his goal being nothing less than the liberation of his homeland, Venezuela. The New Granada Congress was reluctant to accede to Bolívar's ambition, however, fearing the overstretching of limited resources. Nonetheless, on May 7, Bolívar at last received orders to march on Venezuela, but then only to free two border provinces, Mérida and Trujillo. On May 14, Bolívar, now a brigadier general and citizen of New Granada, entered Venezuela. In less than 10 days, he was in Mérida, high in the Andes. It was here that Bolívar was first acclaimed "El Liberator." Barely stopping to rest, it was on to Trujillo, where the young general and his army of 700 arrived on June 14. What would eventually be known as the Admirable Campaign had, at least so far, been an unqualified success.

REIGN OF TERROR

The "admirable" campaign, so named for its success in "freeing" new territory for the patriot cause, soon turned into a reign of terror. Monteverde, the chief royalist commander, was quick in allowing his subordinates to kill both belligerents and civilians. One of his officers, Antonio Zuazola, who mutilated, burned, and murdered indiscriminately, supposedly ordered troops to "spare no one over seven years."[5] On the patriot side, Antonio Nicolás Briceño, a neighbor of Bolívar's, offered promotion to his officers and men in return for the heads of Spaniards. Though his macabre policy was disavowed by Bolívar, this did not prevent Briceño (known as *El Diablo*, or "The Devil," among his colleagues) from sending the Liberator the severed head of an elderly Spanish civilian.

It was at this time, upon his capture of Trujillo, that Bolívar's policy of "war to the death" was initiated. Bolívar declared, "Our tolerance is now exhausted, and as our oppressors force us into a mortal war they will disappear from America and our land will be purged of the monsters who

CENTAURS OF THE PLAINS

Llaneros were the first cowboys of the Americas, occupying the vast llanos, or plains, of Venezuela and Colombia, beginning in the mid-sixteenth century. With the coming of the wars for independence, the llaneros were recruited by Spanish forces to fight against the aristocratic creoles that, in many cases, looked down on them as rough, uncouth, mestizos, and peasants. Simón Bolívar, however, realized that the llaneros made great warriors, and thus needed to be recruited to aid in the independence cause.

To win over the llaneros, Bolívar came to live among them, to be as much a centaur as possible. Though slight of build, Bolívar ate, swam, slept, and lived for months on end like a llanero. He endured the hardships of the llanos: heat, cold, storms, high winds, and hours in the saddle. The Liberator's efforts paid off; the llaneros eventually became staunch allies in the fight to rid northern South America of Spanish rule.

Today, the llaneros still ride the llanos as modern cowboys. According to Bonnie Hamre, "The llaneros are proud of their hard lives, the true cowboys live close to nature from cradle to grave. They break in fresh horses each year, releasing them to run wild when the rains come. Their rich folklore is revealed in legends and stories, and in poignant songs accompanied by the strum of the cuatro guitar or the lilting rhythms of the Venezuelan harp."*

* Bonnie Hamre. *Llaneros—Cowboys of Colombia and Venezuela.* http://gosouth america.about.com/od/venartandculture/a/llaneros.htm.

infest it. Our hatred will be implacable; the war will be to the death."[6]

On June 15, Bolívar went even further, stating, "Any Spaniard who does not collaborate against tyranny in favour of the just cause, actively and effectively, shall be considered an enemy and punished as a traitor to the country, and in consequence shall be inescapably executed. . . . Spaniards and Canarians, know that you will die, even if you are simply neutral, unless you actively espouse the liberation of America."[7]

Thus fear became a weapon of war, both for the Spaniards and the patriots. There is little doubt that the former were, as Robert Harvey declared, "fiendishly inhuman in their cruelty. They raped women, then tied them to their hammocks and set fires under them, literally roasting them to death. They peeled prisoners' feet and made them walk across hot coals; ears were trophies of war."[8] Yet, Bolívar's policy of, as Harvey put it, "legitimized slaughter," was in many ways no better and would, in time, prove counterproductive. "This was not a proclamation [war to the death] issued by a young hot-head in the thick of fighting, or the ranting of a murderous local despot. It was the calculated authorization of racial murder, even of the innocent, to secure the advantage of his own side."[9] The line between just and unjust retribution was proving to be a thin one indeed.

MAN ON HORSEBACK

There was no stopping Bolívar now. Up and over the cordillera (mountain ranges), his army of nearly 2,000 went, surprising and ambushing royalist forces where they found them. In one notable battle, on the plains of Taguanes, in late July, Bolívar ordered his cavalry and infantry to mount double. Riding two men to a horse, the patriots galloped around the enemy. Then, just at the crucial moment, the infantry dismounted and charged ahead with cavalry support. The combined infantry-cavalry column cut the Spanish units to pieces.

Bolívar occupied Valencia, Venezuela's second city, on August 2. Two days later, he entered La Victoria, where he found a royalist capitulation commission (hurriedly sent from Caracas) waiting to negotiate with him.

Bolívar, never self-effacing or bashful, now took pen to paper and wrote to the Congress at Tunja, summarizing his recent triumphs. "During the three months that I waged war in Venezuela, I did not go into an action from which we did not emerge victorious and from each encounter, by surprising the enemy through unexpected marches, I obtained every possible advantage, while the valor of my soldiers struck them with terror."[10] Bolívar pointed out that in addition to insuring the principal objective of his mission (to redeem Venezuela from servitude), he had succeeded in taking large supplies of arms and munitions from the enemy. Both his genius and audacity were on full display.

On August 6, 1813, Bolívar made his triumphant entry into Caracas. The returning hero was carried forth in a carriage drawn by 12 beautiful young maidens, who were all elegantly dressed in white, adorned with the national colors, and all selected from the first families of Caracas.[11] That evening, Bolívar danced until midnight at a ball given in his honor. It was at this time that the Liberator began his relationship with Josefina Machado, one of the 12 girls in white. Though no raving beauty, the 20-year-old would become the Liberator's acknowledged mistress for the next five years.

Over his lifetime, it is said that Bolívar received more than 2,000 love letters from fawning, admiring women. He was a man that clearly knew how to mix warring, politics, and the pleasures of life. He would become what Slatta and De Grummond declared, "The quintessential 'man on horse-back,' the model of the powerful Spanish American leader who inspired a host of imitators, some for better but many for worse."[12] John Lynch further elaborated, "Glory on the campaign, power in government, a woman in his bed—Bolívar took it all as his due."[13]

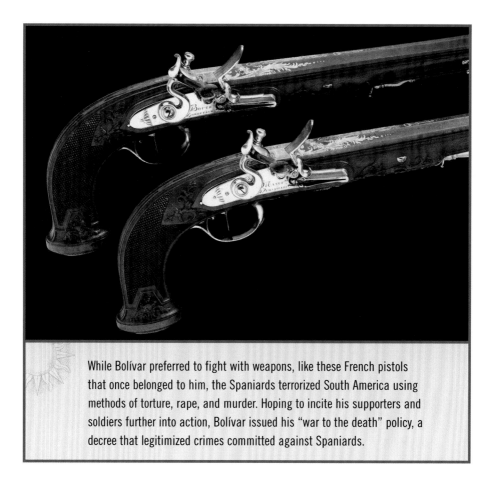

While Bolívar preferred to fight with weapons, like these French pistols that once belonged to him, the Spaniards terrorized South America using methods of torture, rape, and murder. Hoping to incite his supporters and soldiers further into action, Bolívar issued his "war to the death" policy, a decree that legitimized crimes committed against Spaniards.

The Liberator soon turned to that power in government, pledging, in this Second Republic, constitutional rule for Venezuela. While he assured the citizens of Caracas that, "Nothing shall turn me from my first and only intentions—your glory and liberty,"[14] Bolívar, nonetheless, refused to fall into the federalist trap. He retained supreme executive and legislative powers.

All of Venezuela was not yet the Liberator's, however. The bulk of the royalist army remained intact at numerous points on the coast and in the country's vast llanos (plains). From the llanos would emerge a particularly fearsome patriot opponent—José Tomás Rodríguez Boves, a "land pirate" of incredible daring and effective leadership.

DEVILS ON HORSEBACK

The llanos are vast, tropical grassland, occupying half the land-mass of Venezuela. The Andes on the east descend to forest, then to the llanos, which feed the great basin of the Orinoco. The region is characterized by extreme climate change. In the dry season, the torrid heat easily exceeds 100°F (37.7°C). During the rainy season (June to October), the whole terri-tory usually floods because its baked soil cannot hold water. Parts of the llanos can become inundated with up to a meter of floodwater, making travel for both horse and man nearly impossible.

Before the Spanish arrived, the area was barely populated. But with the introduction of horses and cattle in the sixteenth century, tremendous herds grew and spread. By the second decade of the nineteenth century, over a million cattle and an equal number of horses roamed the plains, pretty much for the taking.

It wasn't long before the animals of the llanos began to provide a living for those willing to endure the land's hard-ships. Known as llaneros, or plainsmen, these tough, poor, often ex-slaves rode horses and herded cattle. They were the cowboys of Venezuela. But, as Robert Harvey pointed out, there was nothing romantic about them. "Largely black, Indian or mestizos, they rode mostly naked except for rough trousers, and broad-brimmed hats to protect them from the sun. Their diet consisted of raw beef, tied to their saddles in strips and salted by the sweat of their horses, washed down by the brack-ish water of the *llanos*. . . . Their roughness ensured they were in fact subject to no one except their own local leaders."[15]

One such *caudillo* (chieftain) to emerge was Boves. He was a born fighter, with a streak of psychopathic cruelty. By 1813, the 31-year-old white Spaniard was raising thousands of colored llaneros for the royalist cause. "White lands to the blacks"[16] was his rallying cry, knowing full well the resentment his men felt toward creole slaveholders. Promising his follow-ers plunder and rape, Boves ranged wide and far, taking what did not belong to him and literally slaughtering anyone—man, woman, or child—along the way.

Forming what became known as the Legion of Hell, Boves and his lance-wielding llaneros engaged patriot forces on numerous fronts, including those led by Bolívar. Of Boves, the Liberator would declare, "He was not nurtured with the delicate milk of a woman but with the blood of tigers and the furies of hell."[17] In battle after battle, in the closing months of 1813, the patriots experienced defeat after defeat at the hands of Boves, whose army had risen to 10,000. Increasingly, the patriots found themselves fighting on too many fronts. "Bolívar and his army fought magnificently against this sudden surfeit [overabundant supply] of challenges, tearing up and down the central highlands and valleys of the country, fending off one attack after another," Robert Harvey wrote. "At Carabobo he personally defeated the Spanish and chased them back once again into Puerto Cabello. But from their strongholds in the coastal lowlands, from the baked badlands of the *llanos* and from the humid lowlands of the east, the provocations proved remorseless."[18]

It was, once again, simply too much for the patriot cause. Unable to obtain wide popular backing, Bolívar, on June 15, 1814, was forced to flee Caracas, along with 20,000 terrified whites. It was the end of the Second Republic, and once again Bolívar stood desperate and disgraced.

Defeat
and Victory

For Bolívar, a pattern of defeat, followed by victory, followed by defeat was now apparent. It is remarkable that he was so capable of rising, phoenix-like, after each seemingly fatal setback. Such was Bolívar's personality, reflecting blind optimism on the one hand, near delusion on the other, that he was determined never to give up. "I promise you beloved compatriots," the Liberator announced on his departure for New Granada in early September 1814, "that this august title [Liberator] which your gratitude bestowed upon me when I broke your chains will not be in vain. . . . Do not compare your physical strength with the enemy's for spirit is not to be compared with matter. You are men, they are beast, you are free, they are slaves. Fight and you shall win. God grants victory to the steadfast."[1]

As Bolívar sailed, Boves, leading hundreds of followers, advanced on the town of Cumana. Here he slaughtered a thousand civilians in a bizarre "fiesta," where the sadistic llanero gathered women for a dance, and at the same time dragged their men off to be executed. The wives were forced to perform for his men, before being raped and killed. Mercifully, in the battle to follow at Urica, Boves was killed when his stomach was cut open by a patriot lance. Yet Tomás Francisco Morales, Boves's successor, was to prove no less cruel. In another operation, he captured patriot José Félix Ribas, shot him, dismembered his body, and cooked his head in oil. The "trophy" was taken to Caracas, where it was displayed, topped with a red cap.[2]

On September 20, 1814, despite the defeat of the Second Republic, Bolívar arrived in Cartagena to a hero's welcome. Within weeks, he left the port city for Tunja, in the eastern highlands. As Bolívar approached the capital, he encountered a division of supporters under the leadership of Rafael Urdaneta. The men, delirious with joy, rushed to meet Bolívar and escort him into the city. On November 24, the Liberator gave an account of his successes and failures to the New Granadian Congress. Camilo Torres y Tenorio, president of the Congress, interrupted Bolívar and declared, "General, your country is not vanquished while you have the sword. With it you will return to redeem Venezuela again from her oppressors. The Congress of New Granada will give you its protection because it is satisfied with your record. You may have been an unfortunate solider, but you are a great man."[3]

His support seemingly assured, Bolívar nonetheless faced daunting obstacles to unifying New Granada and retaking his homeland. Upon the defeat of Napoléon I in Europe, Ferdinand VII regained the throne in Spain, vowing to put an end, once and for all, to this independence nonsense in Spanish America. The king appointed 37-year-old General Pablo Morillo to lead an army of war-weary troops to Venezuela. On February 17, 1815, a flotilla of 12,254 men departed Cádiz. With 42 transports and 5 escorting warships, this would be the largest expedition Spain ever sent to the New World.

Fed up with the uprisings and the ongoing success of Bolívar, King Ferdinand VII of Spain sent his forces on a mission to stamp out any notions of independence in the New World. With 42 transports and five warships, an offensive campaign was launched from the Spanish port city of Cadiz (*above*) in 1815.

NO LACK OF VISION

By the spring of 1815, New Granada was plunging into civil war. Though Bolívar led troops to numerous small-scale victories over Spanish garrisons, it was apparent that Cartagena, controlled by rival Manuel del Castillo, would not accept the "foreign" Liberator's authority. Recognizing that the time was anything but advantageous to his vision for recapturing Venezuela, Bolívar, with a sad heart, departed Cartagena on a vessel belonging to English merchant Maxwell Hyslop. The once wealthy creole landowner, now almost penniless, arrived in Jamaica to self-imposed exile, on May 14, 1815.

Taking up residency in a rundown boardinghouse in Kingston, the capital of Jamaica, Bolívar found himself in desperate straits. In a letter to Hyslop begging for financial support, he threatened suicide: "I don't have a penny now. I have sold the little silver I brought. I have no other hope than to seek your favor. Without it, desperation will force me to end my days in a violent manner, in order to avoid the cruel humiliation of begging for help from men harder than their gold."[4]

Bolívar need not have contemplated suicide, for others were hard at work plotting his murder. In one notable effort, a servant, having been bribed with Spanish gold, tried to assassinate Bolívar while he slept in his hammock. Unbeknownst to the servant, however, Bolívar had risen earlier and was in the arms of a mistress when the assassin came to kill him. An exhausted bodyguard, seeking respite in Bolívar's vacant hammock, was the unfortunate victim.

It was at this time that fortune literally struck the ever-amorous and lucky Bolívar. Relief for his desperate financial situation came from Julia Cobier, a Dominican creole lady rebounding from an unsatisfactory love affair. "They fell upon each other in mutual need, as sometimes happens between two people who have experienced horrors or personal sadness," wrote Robert Harvey. "She had the added attraction for Bolívar of being wealthy, and beneath her ministrations his spirit began to revive."[5]

Bolívar was so refreshed from his love affair that he sat down to write what was to be his most famous pronouncement, the "Letter from Jamaica." Written to Hyslop and dated September 6, 1815, the 8,000-word missive roamed widely over a variety of subjects. "Let us strive not for the best [government] but for the most likely of attainment,"[6] Bolívar instructed his reader. The Liberator foresaw a great federation of Hispanic American republics, which would command the same respect as European nations. Bolívar even anticipated the building of a canal in Panama: "The British can acquire (in return for aid) the provinces of Panama and Nicaragua, forming with these countries the centre of the world's commerce by means of canals."[7] Even in exile, Bolívar displayed great vision.

UNMITIGATED DISASTER

Morillo was not idle during Bolívar's absence from the mainland. In mid-August, the supreme royalist commander arrived at Cartagena to take an active part in its siege. Although enemy bombardments had done their damage to patriot positions within the city, there was little left for Morillo to do but wait out its inhabitants. It would be the virtual starvation of the city's residents that eventually destroyed all resistance. "By the end of November the few foodstuffs still available were being sold by speculators at astronomic prices; those who could not buy were reduced to devouring rats or strips of leather soaked in water; thousands had already died," wrote David Bushnell. "In the end, anyone who could pile onto a few corsair ships to try to escape to the West Indies, and around six hundred managed to reach Haiti and Jamaica without dying at sea or being captured by the enemy. When the army of Fernando VII finally entered Cartagena on 6 December, it viewed a gruesome cityscape of living skeletons and unburied corpses. A third of Cartagena's roughly 15,000 inhabitants had died during the siege."[8]

It was at this time that Bolívar, answering a call to return to Cartagena to restore unity and provide leadership to the patriot cause, encountered a ragtag squadron fleeing the fallen city. He ordered his small boat to follow them to Haiti, which formed the western half of Hispaniola. Bolívar, much to his surprise and relief, was warmly greeted by the Haitian president, Alexandre Pétion, who presided over a free population of ex-slaves that had rebelled in 1804. Bolívar was also welcomed by a Jewish merchant from Curaçao, Luis Brión, whose admiration for the Liberator and his cause knew no bounds. He promised Bolívar an arsenal of "15,200 muskets, 2,500 musket locks, 400 carbines, 300 sabers, 200 pairs of pistols, 200 quintals [20,000 pounds] of powder, and 3 printing presses."[9] Brión also had a number of ships at his disposal, including a small frigate and a 24-gun corvette. For the first time, Bolívar actually had a naval force he could deploy. The Liberator was overcome with gratitude and joy.

On July 6, 1816, Bolívar, with 1,000 men, landed at the small town of Ocumare, on the northeastern coast of Venezuela. Tragically, this new attempt at retaking the homeland would be an unmitigated disaster. Most of Bolívar's men, dispatched to the interior, were cut off by the Spanish army. Bolívar's ships fled in panic, leaving him and a handful of men stranded. And, most ominously, in-fighting developed between patriot leaders. When rival officers refused to acknowledge Bolívar's authority, he had to fight to the beach for escape, with sword in hand. "Bolívar was now but a man of straw, a figure of world vision and grandiose rhetoric who could not command respect among his own men, much less make an impression on the enemy," wrote Robert Harvey. "A lesser spirit would have been shattered."[10]

JAMAICA LETTER

Simón Bolívar was not only an extraordinary military genius leading the fight for northern South American independence; he was the intellectual force behind the very revolution. In his Jamaica Letter, written while in exile in Kingston, on September 6, 1815, Bolívar clearly states why the creole class should give up everything in a fight for freedom from Spain. In particular, he bemoans the lack of preparation his countrymen have been given in the art of governing:

> "From the beginning we were plagued by a practice that in addition to depriving us of the rights to which we were entitled left us in a kind of permanent infancy with respect to public affairs. If we had even been allowed to manage the domestic aspects of our internal administration, we would understand the processes and mechanisms of public affairs; then we would enjoy the personal esteem in the eyes of the public that derives from a certain automatic respect so necessary to maintain during revolutions."

It is this lack of knowledge and experience in governing that would account for Bolívar's more authoritarian tendencies in the years to come.

But not Bolívar. To his surprise and relief, the Liberator, upon his return to Haiti, was greeted, not with derision and contempt, but with honor and sympathy. For many on the island and elsewhere, Bolívar was still the best and the only hope for redeeming the patriot cause.

UP THE ORINOCO RIVER

On the last day of 1816, Bolívar returned to the mainland and to the port city of Barcelona, Venezuela. He would never leave South America again.

Caracas, as always, was the Liberator's main objective. This time, however, he got only as far as Clarines before being forced back to Barcelona. Bolívar had no support. The caudillos (chiefs) he thought he could count on, and for whom he begged assistance, were not forthcoming. Most were operating independently in the east, in Guayana, and had no intention of coming to Bolívar's aid. One in particular, Manuel Piar, was hoping to see Bolívar defeated, all the better to take his place as the new Liberator. Without caudillo assistance, Bolívar was obliged to abandon any hope of taking Caracas. The northern coast of Venezuela was simply too strongly garrisoned and blockaded by Spaniards. Bolívar would need a new strategy if he was to successfully launch a Third Venezuela Republic.

To this end, Bolívar (and what men he had) now marched into Guayana, deep into the hinterland of the vast Orinoco basin. One of South America's great rivers, the Orinoco—huge, sluggish, and brown—winds its way over 1,500 miles (2,414 km), from its source in the Serra Parima on Venezuela's border with Brazil to a 400-mile-wide (643.7-km-wide) delta at the Caribbean. The Orinoco artery was home to a thriving contraband trade in hides, horses, and cattle from the llanos. For Bolívar, it was seen as a possible springboard for attack into the heart of Venezuela, and at the same time as a barrier against defeat. Furthermore, taking control of the region would provide export wealth in the form of livestock. With such income, the patriots could purchase badly needed war materials. It was a brilliant strategy.

Angostura, 250 miles (402.3 km) upriver from the Orinoco delta, was Bolívar's major objective. An elegant Spanish city on the edge of the llanos, Angostura boasted cobbled streets, a beautiful cathedral, and a fair climate. It would be an ideal base for further patriot penetration into Venezuela.

In early 1817, Piar laid siege to Angostura. Admiral Brión, reaching the Orinoco in early July with a flotilla of schooners and brigantines, cut off any royalist attempt to sail upriver. On July 17, Angostura surrendered. Though Piar had paved the way to victory, and Brión provided the finishing blow, Bolívar led the way. "He had shared all the privations of his troops, had exposed himself to grave dangers—once spending the night immersed in a small lake to escape enemy pursuers—and he more than anyone, had orchestrated the campaign," wrote David Bushnell. "It was a personal triumph for Bolívar."[11] The Liberator's new, grand strategy seemed to be paying off.

BOLÍVAR AND THE LLANEROS

Bolívar's new scheme was augmented by a refusal of Morillo and the royalists to recognize the contributions made by the likes of Boves, despicable as he was, to the Spanish cause. Upon his arrival in Venezuela, Morillo was quick to restore the old social structure and property rights—including slavery. The creole elite, weary of the death and destruction the independence movement had produced so far, would have, in many cases, been content with the reestablishment of their former status and privileges. But Morillo would have none of it. He went so far as to forbid his officers to marry creole women. The Spanish wanted nothing less than a restoration of an obsolete system of absolute monarchy, with peninsular Spaniards at the top, creoles under their thumb, and the colored of Venezuela, as always, at the bottom.

Upon arriving in Cartagena, Spanish general Pablo Morillo blockaded the city and waited for its occupants to either flee or starve. When some attempted to board ships headed for Haiti or Jamaica, Spanish forces were able to capture them. Those involved in the revolution, like Pantaleon German Ribon and his men, were later executed (*above*).

Bolívar sought to take advantage of royalist interagency by offering llaneros and slaves a stake in the revolution. But to gain their support for his cause, the Liberator first had to suppress dissension within his own ranks. Bolívar had to gain the confidence of rival caudillos, particularly Manuel Piar.

A contemporary account describes Piar as "young, of medium height and a martial air; brave, impetuous and of lightning speed in action; terse in his views, arrogant and impulsive almost to madness, he had a furious temper to the extent that he sometimes apologized to subordinates he had offended."[12] In a sense, Piar saw himself as another Boves, a leader of the blacks, albeit for the patriot cause.

To gain the respect of the llaneros, Bolívar would have to overcome his own persona. To that end, the Liberator sought to excel in all that the llaneros prided themselves in. He sat around their campfires and sang their songs. He shared their privations, sleeping in a hammock or on the ground. And Bolívar insisted on grooming his own horse, a point of honor among the llaneros.

In one attempt to display his manhood, Bolívar engaged a llanero commander in a swimming contest. With his hands voluntarily tied behind him, Bolívar outswam the commander to a designated marker 150 yards away (137.1 meters). In another instance of machismo, Bolívar vaulted over his own horse, from its rear, to over its head. "You must not believe that this is of no importance for a man who commands others," Bolívar was to write of the event later. "In everything, if possible, he must demonstrate his superiority to those who must obey. It's the method of establishing lasting prestige and indispensable for those who occupy the first rank in society and particularly for someone commanding an army."[13]

Bolívar was also convinced that a leader must stand up to any risk to his authority. In Piar, Bolívar saw such a peril, particularly when the latter threatened to replace him on racial grounds—to, in the Liberator's mind, plunge the patriot cause into a civil war of creole against *casta* (a member of the lower classes). Bolívar, seeking to make an example of Piar, had him captured, tried as a traitor to the cause, and executed. Piar represented regionalism, personalism, and black revolution, according to John Lynch. Bolívar, on the other hand, stood for centralism, constitutionalism, and race harmony.[14]

Cordillera Conquest

Although Bolívar had, in Manuel Piar, eliminated a formidable caudillo rival, he soon confronted another in the tough and skillful José Antonio Páez. The llanos chieftain was described by Daniel O'Leary, a lifelong Bolívar confidant, as "Of medium height, robust, and well-formed, though the lower part of his body did not match his big torso . . . lively brown eyes, straight nose with wide apertures, thick lips. . . . His clear white but deeply tanned skin indicated good health."[1]

The illiterate Páez suffered from epilepsy, which, according to Slatta and De Grummond, only added to his mystique. "Sometimes in the heat of battle, he fell from his horse, helpless, glassy-eyed, and foaming at the mouth. At those times, his bodyguard, Pedro Camejo, a large Afro-Venezuelan called 'El Negro Primero' (The First Black), would rescue Páez."[2]

The llanero was famous for marching at night, all the better to go unobserved and avoid the heat of day. A 60-mile

(96.5-km) ride was not uncommon. His men could advance and retreat with amazing rapidity. Though unread, Páez was considered an astute and intelligent man, imbued with the admired Spanish characteristic of *hombria* ("manliness"). While Boves commanded a large army of llaneros against the patriots, Páez, operating out of his western llanos base, would do the same against the royalists. Both men were vicious and untamed, and regarded plunder as their right.

Bolívar needed Páez, yet feared him as a rival for control of the independence movement. On January 31, 1818, at San Juan de Payara, the caudillo and the Liberator met for the first time. "The two dismounted and embraced. They stood about the same height, five feet six inches [167.6 cm]. Bolívar marveled at the lionlike head, the fair, sunburned skin, the broad shoulders, and the massive chest of the twenty-seven-year-old master of the *llanos*. Páez saw black eyes, penetrating and restless like those of an eagle, hands and feet as dainty as those of a woman, and a slight body that was never still."[3]

Both commanders committed to a mutual effort at defeating the enemy they faced. Bolívar moved his army up to San Juan de Payara. On February 6, 5,000 patriots mounted and headed north to Calabozo, 100 miles (160.9 km) away.

To reach their destination, the forces would have to ford the fast-flowing Apure River. Bolívar turned to Páez and asked, "How are we going to cross?"[4] Páez, in response, took 50 men into the water, swam up to a royalist camp on the far bank, and boarded enemy gunboats. Most of the royalists plunged into the water in a desperate attempt at escape.

On February 12, the combined armies of Páez and Bolívar reached the outskirts of Calabozo, a city named "jail" because its walled city was considered by many to be impenetrable. Time would tell.

THE BRITISH ARE COMING

The coming months would not go well for the patriot cause. Indeed, Bolívar would soon experience his greatest defeat to date, one that would drive him to the edge of sanity.

Bolívar forged an alliance with General José Antonió Páez, a sturdy and effective leader of the llaneros. Although the two fought side by side for independence, Bolívar feared Páez would become a political rival after the revolution was over.

Though Bolívar and Páez, upon reaching Calabozo, were quick to surround Morillo and his forces to the point of demanding the royalist's surrender, the clever Morillo soon slipped away to regroup at the edge of the cordillera. Páez refused to pursue him, knowing that he and his llaneros would be out of their element in mountainous terrain. Instead, he turned south to San Fernando, leaving Bolívar to go it alone.

It was at this time that the Liberator, seeming forever fixated on Caracas, took a bold but foolish risk. Without Páez, Bolívar headed straight for the Venezuelan capital. On his way, at La Puerta, he met up with Morillo's second in command, La Torre, and his vast, well-equipped, and rested forces. "There the whole Patriot army disintegrated in a headlong retreat amidst appalling bloodshed, leaving a thousand dead, many of them officers," wrote Robert Harvey. "Bolívar himself only narrowly escaped to Calabozo, where the pitiful remnants of his army gathered. It was the most comprehensive military defeat he had yet suffered, and almost entirely self-inflicted: it had been madness, tactically and strategically, to attempt, with an inferior force, to charge straight into the heart of the enemy, on their terrain, where they had vastly superior armies."[4]

Bolívar was near derangement. "He fell ill—feverish, exhausted, depressed, unable to mount a horse because of boils on his thighs."[5] Yet, though the Liberator had lost virtually his entire army along with 3,000 horses, he would continue the struggle. On May 24, the indomitable Bolívar set sail down the Orinoco to Angostura. Over the next year, he would again raise a new army.

Bolívar would do so not only among llaneros but also from foreign legionaries who were recruited from as far away as Scotland, Ireland, Germany, France, Italy, Holland, Russia, Poland, Canada, the United States, and, most notably, England. With the defeat of Napoléon I and the cessation of European conflicts, tens of thousands of soldiers and sailors were thrown out of work. "The peace threw back on the country [England] an immense number of mariners and soldiers who increased expenditure and made no return by their labors,"[6] reported the *London Chronicle*. It was estimated that close to half a million ex-British soldiers needed to be absorbed by a population of 25 million. "Many of them [soldiers] had been engaged in military work for so long that they were unfit for civilian pursuits. Some of them looked longingly to other parts of the world for an opportunity for continuing their military careers."[7]

Bolívar's agents, operating in Europe since 1816, lost no time in recruiting unemployed officers and men, promising them pay increases, promotions, and, of course, glory in the cause of Latin American independence. The Liberator felt that the arrival of professional soldiers from Europe, infused among the llanero ranks, would provide the fighting edge his army desperately needed. At the very time when all seemed hopeless to the independence cause, boatloads of English mercenaries began arriving to take up arms.

CORDILLERA ORIENTAL

Before Bolívar planned for a new military venture, however, he turned his attention to politics, calling together delegates for a Congress of Angostura, on February 15, 1819. Only 29 representatives arrived from the relatively small areas of the country that the patriots controlled. Nonetheless, the Congress that would elect Bolívar president afforded him the opportunity for yet another pronouncement, to be known thereafter as his Angostura Address. In it, Bolivar reiterated his call for a powerful executive. "Nothing is as dangerous with respect to the people as weakness in the executive power. . . . In a republic, the executive should be the strongest power, because everything conspires against him."[8] Bolívar also called for unity between Venezuela and Colombia. For that to occur, however, a new, truly bold military venture would be required.

On May 23, Bolívar gathered his officers in a hut in the hamlet of Setenta by the Arauca River. They sat on the bleached skulls of bullocks, as no tables and chairs were available. The

Liberator told of his plan to forsake Caracas for the time being and instead surprise the enemy in the Andean mountains of Colombia. "His intention was to move through the uninhabited south-western *llanos* into the foothills of the Andes and up over the top of the Cordillera Oriental itself at one of its highest points—and then descend to battle with the enemy."[9] His officers thought Bolívar was mad. Yet, when Colonel Rooke of the British Albion Legion stood up and announced he would follow Bolívar all the way to Cape Horn if necessary, the others relented. It would be one of the epic marches in history.

"No man but Bolívar would have dreamed of that march, nor been able to lead his men through it," wrote historian Marion Lansing. "For one week the march across the flooded *llanos* went on, with men lost in the rushing rivers as they attempted to cross them, with cattle lost, and clothes becoming damp rags in the tropical heat and humidity. All the days Bolívar rode up and down the long line on his horse, encouraging men who faltered, lifted those who fell, snatching a man from the river as he was attacked by a devouring alligator, always pressing on."[10]

Then the country changed to green, jungle-covered hills and the mountains of the cordillera. "The cold winds swept down on those men of the plains who had never before been off their low, grassy lands and were now almost naked after the wet march behind them. They felt the dreaded mountain sickness which caught their lungs so that they could not breathe, and gave them nausea and a numbing pain in the head and limbs so that they could hardly move. . . . Horses lay down to die, but men kept on, beating their freezing hands and feet."[11]

Then, it was on through the highest of Andean passes, Páramo de Pisba, at 13,000 feet (3,962.4 m). Bolívar's officers only agreed to go forward because the alternative, going back through the floodwaters of the llanos, was worse. Of the 2,000 men (and some women) who left the llanos on May 26, 800 perished. Virtually all animals—horses, mules, and cattle—were lost. The march did, indeed, seem like madness.

BATTLE OF BOYACÁ

From Páramo de Pisba, Bolívar and his ragged band descended into the village of Soatá, at 8,000 feet (2,438.4 m). The inhabitants were at first terrified of the desperate patriots. But soon enough, a festival of support was organized. At a church gathering on July 24, 1819, "Each person was obliged to donate every piece of clothing except the minimum needed to cover his or her nakedness. . . . The sacrificed clothing served the Patriots well. In subsequent battles some soldiers fought wearing women's blouses."[12]

The first few military engagements were indecisive. So, too, was the battle of July 25, at Pantano de Vargas. Yet the psychological impact was great. Although the royalists succeeded in securing the high ground, a considerable tactical

ANDES MOUNTAINS

The Andean mountain system, which Bolívar and his men found as difficult to subdue as any human adversary, ranges more than 5,000 miles (8,046.7 km) in length, down the entire western South American continent, along the Pacific coast. The Andes cut through seven South American countries: Argentina, Chile, Bolivia, Peru, Ecuador, Colombia, and Venezuela. Earthquakes and active volcanoes are common throughout the mountains. Only the Himalayas, in Asia, are loftier than the Andes, where snowcapped peaks of more than 22,000 feet (6,705.6 m) are not uncommon. The waters of the Andes reach the Orinoco, the Amazon, and the Río de la Plata.

In Colombia, the Andes split into three distinct ranges, known as the Cordillera (cord). The western (or occidental) range runs between the coast and the Cauca River. The central range stretches between the Cauca and Magdalena Rivers. The eastern (or oriental) parallels the Magdalena River. Bolívar soon discovered that to defeat the Spanish, he first had to conquer the Andes.

The Battle of Boyacá (*above*) was brief, but incredibly important to Bolívar's cause. With the victory, patriot forces easily overtook Bogotá, preventing further royalist advances. Thanks to this strategic win, Bolívar and his men were able to defeat their enemies.

advantage, the patriots fought bravely to a draw. Colonel Rooke, however, sustained a devastating blow when his arm was shattered by a musket ball—necessitating its amputation. As the story goes, when the arm fell, he seized it in his other hand, lifted it up, and shouted in Spanish, "Long live the fatherland." The surgeon asked him in English, "Which country, Ireland or England?" Rooke replied, "The one which is to give me burial."[13] Rooke died three days later. Of the British warrior, Bolívar proclaimed: "To him I owe all my good fortune in New Granada and to him Venezuela is indebted for the preservation of her president and will hereafter have mainly to attribute her liberty."[14]

Bolívar's goal was, of course, Santaé, soon to be renamed Bogotá. With new recruits, some conscripted on pain of execution, the Liberator made his way south, to Tunja. With a good night's rest, on the morning of August 7, 2,800 patriots set out to meet 2,700 royalists, led by José María Barreiro, at the bridge of Boyacá. At about two in the afternoon, what was to become known as the Battle of Boyacá got under way.

Within two hours, it was all over. A demoralized Barreiro surrendered along with most of his officers. One prisoner turned out to be the very officer, Francisco Vinoni, whose betrayal led to Bolívar's loss of Puerto Cabello in 1812. The Liberator lost no time in exacting revenge. He had the man hanged, with his body left dangling in the plaza of the village of Ventaquemada.

Though the Battle of Boyacá was of short duration, it was the most important of all Bolívar's victories. "Prior to Boyacá, he [Bolívar] had lost about as many battles as he had won; from now on, he would go from triumph to triumph, with only occasional and transitory reverses."[15]

GRAN COLOMBIA

Bolívar entered Bogotá a hero, on August 10, 1819, three days after his victory at Boyacá. The resident viceroy, Juan Sámano, fearing that the Liberator's "war to the death" was still in effect, fled in terror, along with the Spanish garrison and the entire governing class. According to an eyewitness, "They . . . abandoned their homes and their shops, which sudden converts to the Patriot cause [looters] took over, and they abandoned old people, fathers, wives and children in desolate groups, not daring to look back, so as not to lose a moment, in fear of their lives as refugees . . . Samano . . . fled dressed as a peasant of the savannah, mounted on a fine horse, preceded by a huge escort of cavalry, which pushed aside the wretched refugees, leaving them enveloped in clouds of dust from the galloping horses."[16]

The patriot victory at Boyacá provided a tremendous psychological lift to the independence cause. Hundreds flocked to join Bolívar's army. And, most telling, there were many Spaniards who now saw retention of their empire as all but hopeless. The Marqués de La Puerta, commander of Spanish forces in northern Spanish America, wrote to Madrid that,

"This disgraceful attack [Boyacá] hands to the rebels, in addition to New Granada, many ports on the southern coast, where they will gather their pirates. . . . Bolívar in one day has finished the efforts of five years of campaigning, and in a single battle has reconquered what the King's troops have won in many fights."[17]

Bolívar returned to Angostura in December, leaving his trusted lieutenant, Francisco de Paula Santander, as vice president of New Granada. Before departing, however, Bolívar enjoined Santander not to take reprisals. The vice president immediately had 38 royalists shot in the back. Bolívar may have retreated from his "war to the death," but not Santander.

After three days of nonstop celebrating in Angostura, Bolívar, on December 14, attended an extraordinary session of Congress. A 21-gun salute marked the Liberator's entry. Addressing the delegates, Bolívar got right to the point. He told the multitude that it was time for Venezuela and New Granada to unite. Indeed, Bolívar proposed that a third country, Quito (Ecuador), be included. All present agreed. Thus, what in retrospect would become known as Gran Colombia was born.

As entities, Venezuela, New Granada, and Quito were simply dissolved. The entire country of Gran Colombia was divided into provinces, with strong, central control emanating from Bogotá. The Congress established the rule of free birth, whereby any child of a slave mother would from now on be free. Indian tribute was abolished. The delegates eliminated all religious censorship, except for editions of the Holy Scripture. Members of Congress were said to have wept for joy at what their liberal actions foretold.

This was a heady time for the 36-year-old Liberator. It was the height of his political and military glory. However, much remained to be done. Bolívar had been here before, more than once, and lost it all. The war for true, lasting independence was yet to be won.

6

Venezuelan Triumph

On December 17, 1819, Simón Bolívar, at the insistence of the Angostura Congress, assumed the de facto presidency of Colombia, or, more precisely, became the new country's liberator president. Then, on Christmas Eve, he left for a three-and-a-half month journey to Bogotá, arriving on March 20, 1820. Bolívar didn't stay long in the Andean Highlands, heading almost immediately to Cúcuta, 300 miles (482.8 km) to the north on the border between New Granada and Venezuela. It was here that the Liberator intended to build the capital of the "united realms," a city he hoped to rename Las Casas, in honor of the great Spanish monk Bartolomé de las Casas.

While in Cúcuta, Bolívar's routine was rather predictable. He would usually awake at 6:00 A.M., then stroll to the stables to see that his horses were being well taken care of. Returning to his room, he would read until 9:00 A.M., at which time his breakfast was served. It was then down to business. Bolívar would take reports from his secretary of war and his chief of staff. He would dictate letters to his two secretaries and then read until 5:00 P.M., when dinner was provided.

NOTABLE INFLUENCES

Simón Bolívar had many friends, cohorts, aides, and other individuals he came to rely on for comfort, assistance, and advice. Naturally, there were those that started out as trusted advisors, only to turn against the Liberator in later years—Francisco de Paula Santander being the most notable in this regard. Some who began as foes, if not enemies, in time, however, came to be trusted by Bolívar, who would eagerly seek their advice. Of the latter, José Antonio Páez stands out. That said, there were two individuals in particular who played a significant role in Bolívar's early life: one as a nurturing "parent," the other as a stern but effective teacher.

María, Bolívar's mother, could not nurse Bolívar upon his birth, so she handed the task over to a wet nurse named Hipólita, a strong, intelligent, 30-year-old black slave woman. Bolívar, in a letter written to his sister María Antonia, in 1825, said of Hipólita, "I am sending you a letter from my mother, Hipólita, so that you will give her everything she wishes, and so that you will treat her as though she were your own mother. She nourished my life. I know no other parent but her." In 1827, on Bolívar's triumphant return to Caracas, Hipólita was there to greet the Liberator—"her son."

Bolívar, sensitive of the fact that he was never formally educated at the university level, took pains to point out to his critics that he had received a fine early education from tutors, foremost of whom was Simón Carreño Rodríguez. In a letter, also written in 1825, Bolívar recalled his early time with Rodríguez, "It is not true that my education was badly neglected, since my mother and father made every possible effort in order that I might have proper instruction. They secured for me the foremost teachers in my country. Robinson [Rodríguez], whom you know, taught me reading and writing." It was Rodríguez that accompanied Bolívar to Monte Sacro, in Rome, where he witnessed the future Liberator's pledge to free South America from Spanish rule.

Although Bolívar could appreciate a good meal as well as anyone, his dinner table was usually rather frugal: soup, boiled or roasted chicken or beef, simply prepared vegetables, and some sweets. After supper, Bolívar often went for a horseback ride. At 9:00 P.M., after meeting with friends and officers, the Liberator would retire to his bedroom and read some more. Given Bolívar's extraordinary memory, he could often quote full pages of the authors he admired (Montesquieu and Rousseau being his favorites) almost verbatim.

On April 19, 1820, on the tenth anniversary of the revolution (and just a few days after his arrival in Cúcuta), Bolívar issued a proclamation to the army, which ended:

"Soldiers! You have consecrated the most beautiful region of the world to immortality through your glorious victories. On April 19th Colombia was born. Since then you are ten-years-old."[1]

It wasn't all politics and state planning in Cúcuta. Bolívar often thought of Bernardina Ibañez, who, to his irritation, had recently established a relationship with Ambrosio Plaza, evidently choosing a mere colonel over Bolívar, a general. He asked Santander, his vice president, to have a word with the girl, declaring, "I am tired of writing without any reply. Tell her that I too am single and like her more than does Plaza, for I have never been unfaithful." Santander replied, "She has hopes in Plaza and no hopes in the others, including you. Affairs of the heart are difficult to manage from a distance."[2] In truth, Bernardina simply preferred an on-the-spot lover, as opposed to one who would almost always be away, fighting wars and seeking mistresses to relieve his stress. It was a rare rejection for the amorous Liberator.

ARMISTICE

As significant for the patriot cause as the victory at Boyacá was, on January 1, 1820, there occurred an event in Spain that was of equal importance. On that New Year's Day in Cádiz, a regiment revolted. Led by Colonel Rafael Riego, the army, waiting to embark for America, simply refused to board ships and sail. Yellow fever was spreading among the ranks. But the main cause of the mutiny was the desire on the part of the Spanish revolutionaries to end Ferdinand VII's despotic rule and return Spain to the more liberal constitution of 1812. The expedition ready to leave for the Americas would have been larger than the one sent under Morillo in 1815. Fortunately for the cause of South American independence, there would not be, at least in 1820, any further royalist reinforcements coming from Spain.

Furthermore, in response to the revolt, Ferdinand VII capitulated, offering, at least initially, his subjects at home a more liberal constitution than the old one. That move created dissension not only in Spain but also in her possessions throughout the New World. Royalist forces became demoralized, with a serious split occurring between those favoring Ferdinand VII and partisans for the Constitution.

As a part of the new proclamation emanating from Spain, the government in Madrid ordered its generals and viceroys to negotiate with the patriots. The royalists were instructed to offer the republicans political concessions in return for their allegiance to the Spanish Constitution of 1812. Morillo was not happy. "They are fools in Madrid," he told some of his officers. "The king knows nothing of the happenings here. This is worse than humiliating. It is degrading. . . . And how it will amuse Bolívar!"[3]

Bolívar was indeed pleased with the turn of events, and soon began a correspondence with General Morillo. The Liberator made it clear from the start that Colombian independence was not open for discussion. Morillo would have to accept Colombia as an independent country. Bolívar signed all his letters with the title "President of Colombia."

At first, negotiations deadlocked. Then the commissioners representing both sides arranged a six-month truce. Furthermore, both leaders agreed to meet—neither having ever seen the other. On November 27, 1820, in the town of Santa Ana, halfway between the patriot and royalist armies the two men and their entourages approached each other. Morillo, attired in his best uniform, arrived with a staff of no less than 50 officers. Bolívar, dressed casually, approached with but 10 assistants. In response, Morillo dismissed 40 of his men. "Bolívar has outdone me in generosity,"[4] he was to have said, as he ordered his men to ride back to headquarters.

According to O'Leary, forever taking notes, Morillo then inquired, "Which one is Bolívar?" When he found out, Morillo was to have exclaimed, "What, that little man with the blue coat and cap, riding a mule?"[5]

All day the two men talked. And after their banquet that night, slept under the same roof. It was an auspicious start.

BATTLE OF CARABOBO

While the camaraderie between the two generals lasted, the armistice did not. On April 28, 1821, one month before the peace was to expire, both parties "agreed" to resume hostilities. Bolívar had used the lull in fighting to good advantage, however. He gathered widely dispersed contingents into a formidable army, ready to take on the royalists. The Liberator, a superb tactician and strategist, chose San Carlos as his focal point, 150 miles (241.4 km) to the south of Caracas.

To garner men and equipment, Bolívar marched his infantry on foot, with ammunition and other materials traveling by packhorse or mule. Since the army ate almost nothing but beef, a large herd of cattle had to be mobilized and driven along.

The Liberator quickly distributed his forces into three divisions. Páez, now ready for a fight, came with 1,000 infantry men and 1,500 cavalry. He also brought with him 2,000 spare horses and 4,000 head of cattle. The caudillo reached San Carlos in the second week of June. Generals Manuel Cedeño and Ambrosio Plaza also arrived with large contingencies. General Santiago Mariño served as chief of staff. While the patriot army totaled 10,000 at its start, through disease and desertion it was whittled down to 6,500 when it arrived on

General Morillo and Bolívar met to negotiate an end to the war, but the tentative truce broke and fighting continued with the Battle of Carabobo. Bolívar, along with three other generals, led patriot forces to victory and gained freedom for Venezuela. *Above*, Bolívar presents the flag of liberation to his triumphant soldiers.

June 21 at the heights of Buenavista, 3 miles (4.8 km) from the plain of Carabobo, 12 miles (19.3 km) west of Valencia. The Spanish general La Torre, with 5,000 men, was waiting.

The battle of Carabobo began at 11 A.M. on June 24, 1821. It ended before noon. O'Leary outlined the most decisive action: "Avoiding frontal attack, which the Royalist general was expecting, Bolívar sent Páez and a force of Colombian infantry to the left along a narrow defile exposed to enemy fire, with instructions to gain possession of the heights and fall upon the right, and weakest, flank of the Royalist army. Slashing their way through the undergrowth with machetes, the Patriots gained the heights in heavy fighting and with heavy casualties; an attack from the leading Apure battalion had to be backed up with a bayonet charge by the British battalion, and support from two companies of the Tiradores."[6]

Whole royalist battalions soon surrendered, though La Torre and Morales escaped to Puerto Cabello. Heavy losses were suffered by both sides, with the royalists losing over a thousand men, while the patriots saw at least 200 killed, probably more. One patriot casualty of note was Colonel Plaza, Bolívar's rival for the affection of Bernardina.

Bolívar, along with Páez, now headed to Caracas, arriving on June 29. There, he tried to negotiate an armistice with La Torre, but failed. A month later, the Liberator divided Venezuela into three military departments: the East with José Francisco Bermúdez, the Center with José Antonio Páez, and the West with Santiago Mariño. As Boyacá, in 1819, had gained freedom for New Granada, Carabobo, two years later, did the same for Venezuela. And this time the victory was complete. Northern South America had finally won its independence from Spain.

INTERNAL CONFLICTS

"I fear peace even more than I fear war,"[7] Bolívar was to exclaim in a famous treatise written soon after entering Caracas in 1821. The Liberator had good reason for such dread.

In late June, Bolívar began a cordial exchange of letters with La Torre, who was now holed up in Puerto Cabello, though he would soon depart for Cádiz, Spain. Such a courtesy would have been unthinkable a year earlier. Bolívar granted safe passage to any royalist who wished to leave Venezuela, and forbade his troops from taking revenge. It seemed, at least for now, the Liberator's "war to the death" was on hold.

Yet, the conflicting ambitions of his subordinates troubled Bolívar. He spoke of "The terrifying chaos of Patriots, profiteers,

SIMÓN BOLÍVAR ON SLAVERY

Simón Bolívar believed strongly in human equality. Here, in a letter to Francisco de Paula Santander, on April 18, 1820, the Liberator gives his views on the military and political reasons for freeing slaves within the government's jurisdiction:

"The military reasons for ordering the recruitment of slaves are quite obvious. We need strong, hardy men who are accustomed to inclement weather and fatigue, men who will embrace the cause and the career of arms with enthusiasm, men who identify their own cause with the public interest and who value their lives only slightly more than their death.

"The political reasons are even more powerful. . . . The congress has considered the words of Montesquieu: *In moderate governments political freedom makes civil freedom precious, and anyone deprived of the latter still lacks the former: he sees a happy society in which he has no part; he finds security guaranteed for others but not for him. Nothing so lowers us to the condition of beasts as seeing free men but not being one. Such people are enemies of society, and they become dangerous in numbers. It is not surprising that in moderate governments the state has been brought into turmoil by the rebellion of slaves or that this rarely happens in despotic states.*

"It is, then, clearly demonstrated by political maxims based on historical example that a free government that commits the absurdity of maintaining slaves shall be punished by rebellion and in some cases by extermination, as in Haiti."

egotists, whites, blacks, Federalists, centralists, republicans, good and bad aristocrats and the whole mass of hierarchies which subdivide into different parts."[8] Bolívar saw that a descent into factionalism, civil war, and anarchy was a real possibility.

Such factionalism, on a personal level, soon broke out between Bolívar and his vice president in New Granada, Francisco de Paula Santander. Bolívar wanted money, arms, and 5,000 men for an assault on Peru, still firmly in Spanish control. Santander, who considered himself the real ruler of New Granada, with Bolívar a mere ally, would eventually agree to supply aid, though not willingly.

Still, what Bolívar had achieved in the last 22 months (the time between Boyacá and Carabobo) was truly extraordinary. According to Daniel A. Del Rio, a historian who made it a point to personally travel many of the routes Bolívar took in crossing Colombia, "During this period Bolívar, on horseback, crossed and crisscrossed the Andes several times between Bogotá, in the heart of Colombia, and the plains of Venezuela and Angostura. These peregrinations [wanderings] of the Liberator, sometimes accompanied by only a few officers, but more often while mobilizing large contingents of troops, are approximately equivalent in distance covered in those twenty-two and a half months, to that between New York City on the North and Buenos Aires, Argentina. This was accomplished by Bolívar through impassable mule trails and, while on the rivers of the interior, by using the extremely primitive means of fluvial [stream] transportation prevailing there a century and a half ago."[9]

Yet, as great as Bolívar's accomplishments were, nearly a quarter of a million people had perished to achieve Gran Colombia's independence. True, the patriots now controlled the entire Caribbean coast of Colombia, except for Puerto Cabello (the latter was anything but a prize at this time, as an epidemic of "black vomit," or yellow fever, had broken out).

On November 28, 1821, Panama declared her independence from Spanish rule and asked to join Colombia.

Bolívar received congressional permission to liberate the territories still held by Spain. While Bolívar made his way south, another soldier sought to liberate Peru. José de San Martín proclaimed independence in Lima on July 28, 1821, (*above*) but he would need to work with the Liberator to finally conquer Peru.

Santander agreed to guarantee the move. With Panama in patriot hands, the Spanish would have a rough time reinforcing their possessions in Quito or Lima. Bolívar's misgivings aside, in military respects the situation was, indeed, looking up for the independence forces throughout Latin America.

THE LIBERATING LIBERATOR

Before Bolívar could undertake a southern campaign to liberate Quito (Ecuador) and Peru, he first had to set in place a working government for Gran Colombia. It would not be easy. Bolívar might be able to dominate events, but not conditions. Even the Liberator could not reorder society or the economy. "People's lives were conditioned by the societies and economies in which they found themselves and which the war had not basically changed, except, perhaps, for the worse," wrote John Lynch. "As peace loomed his [Bolívar's] forebodings grew."[10]

The Liberator, of course, believed that the only way to secure Gran Colombia's independence was through a strong central government. Independence had released anarchical forces that Bolívar was sure would take over and split the country if the strong hand of authoritarianism was absent.

Bolívar was quick, however, to deny any personal impulse to dictatorship. He disavowed any ambition to be president. "If, to my regret," Bolívar was to have said in response to Congress's insistence on nominating him, "I will always be absent from the capital, or always ill. . . . You tell me that history will say great things about me. I believe that it will say nothing was greater than my renunciation of power and my absolute dedication to the arms that could save the government and the country. History will say, 'Bolívar took over the government to free his countrymen, and when they were free he left them so that they would be ruled by law and not his will.' That is my answer."[11]

Bolívar, above all, sought glory as well as his position in history as a soldier. He did not want to be an administrator. In the battlefield, not in some government office, is where the Liberator wished to be, doing what he did best—liberating. When accepting the presidency of Gran Colombia, Bolívar did so only on the condition that he be allowed at any time to lead an army of liberation to the south. He would leave governing to his vice president, in effect making him acting president, a role the legalistic Santander was only too willing to undertake. "I [Bolívar] am the son of war, the man whom combat has raised to government. . . . A man like me is a dangerous citizen for a popular government, a threat to national sovereignty."[12]

To that end, Congress passed a law granting Bolívar extraordinary powers. He would be allowed to secure the liberation of territories still held by Spain. The Liberator, wanting only to resume his career as such, could hardly wait to be off.

7

Liberator and Protector

With the liberation of Colombia and Venezuela (and their merger into Gran Colombia), some urged Bolívar to retire, to return to his plantation as a gentleman farmer. His job, they said, was done. Of course, the Liberator felt there was still plenty of liberating left to be done in Latin America and, not surprisingly, believed he was the one (perhaps the only one) to do it. True, in the year 1821, Costa Rica, El Salvador, Guatemala, Honduras, Nicaragua, and Peru had declared their independence, though in the case of Peru the declaration meant little because over 20,000 royalist troops were still in control. Bolívar, eager to advance, now set his sights on that important, mineral-rich Spanish stronghold. Yet to get there, he would have to go through Quito (Ecuador); the mountainous, largely poor country would have to be liberated first.

Within the presidency of Quito, only the city of Guayaquil had so far gained independence. A thriving commercial port,

Guayaquil had rebelled against Spanish rule in October 1820, declaring itself an autonomous city-state. Many of its leaders were more than content with its status as such and hoped it would remain that way indefinitely. Others, however, looked forward to a union with Peru. It was far easier to reach Lima (the capital of Peru) by ship than it was to trek over mountains to the city of Quito (the capital), to say nothing of far-off Bogotá. Yet, earlier, in Angostura and again in Cúcuta, the union of Colombia, Venezuela, and Ecuador had been decreed, if not fully accepted by the inhabitants of the three countries. Bolívar would agree to nothing less.

The plan for Ecuadorian liberation was a simple one, though carrying it out would be anything but. General Antonio José de Sucre, Bolívar's young but trusted lieutenant, would lead an expedition up from the south, from Guayaquil. Bolívar would come down from the north, from Bogotá. In March 1822, the Liberator left with 3,000 men.

Of the two, Sucre had the easier time of it. With the aid of several hundred Peruvian troops, the general battled his way to Quito. Upon his arrival, on May 24, 1822, he caused three Spanish companies to flee, and he captured 2,000 men, 1,700 muskets, 14 cannon, and a substantial quantity of ammunition and stores.[1]

Bolívar, upon reaching the area around Popayán, soon found that nature would prove as great an adversary as any royalist army. "Negotiating rope bridges across gaping chasms, climbing precipitous mountain trails, scrambling up bare rocky passes, struggling over icy ledges and ridges—it was like that march across the Cordillera Oriental again, if less fearsome, and longer."[2] The patriots lost one-third of their forces. They would lose another thousand men in the ensuing battle of Bombóná, on April 7, though they would emerge victorious.

With the triumphs of both Sucre and Bolívar, the viceroy fled, in effect, turning over what is today Ecuador to the patriot cause. Bolívar arrived in Quito on June 16, 1822, in one of his biggest triumphal entries yet. The mostly Indian population greeted the Liberator as a god.

MANUELA SÁENZ

It was at this time, with his march into Quito, that Bolívar, almost 40 years old, met the true love of his later life. Though, upon the death of his young wife in 1803, Bolívar had vowed never to remarry, a pledge he would keep, falling in love again always remained a possibility. With Manuela Sáenz de Thorne, he did just that. While fulfilling the role of mistress, Manuela nonetheless provided much more—as a political partner, confidant, spy, and fanatical champion of the patriot cause.

As the Liberator rode in parade down the main street of Quito, a laurel wreath, tossed from a balcony by the then 25-year-old mestiza beauty, Manuela, hit him on the side of the face. Bolívar recoiled, as he shot a hot glance upward. Yet in that instant, the Liberator was transfixed by what he saw. "Their glances mingled in quick passionate understanding, and that exchange, though neither knew it, was to alter the course of history and the fate of nations."[3]

At the city's victory ball that evening, Bolívar was formally introduced to Manuela. "He watched her dance the cotillion and the polonaise, a slim lithe girl, but luxuriously shaped, with a lovely classic oval face, perfect features, a passionate full mouth."[4] Bolívar was mesmerized.

"Suddenly she [Manuela] stepped out alone on the floor, her skirts held high, to dance the ñapanga before the shocked eyes of the gathering—'Not a dance,' remarked one bishop, 'but the resurrection of the flesh'—not a ballroom dance but one for hoi polloi, during fiestas and in chichi beer parlors. Manuela held stuffy conventions in little esteem."[5]

Sometime before daybreak, Bolívar and Manuela disappeared. No one knew where the two had gone. Yet by the full light of day, all the tongues of Quito were wagging, from salons to servants' quarters, to the marketplaces.

There was just one problem—Manuela was a married woman. Born the illegitimate daughter of a Spanish business-man who was married with four children, Manuela was soon hustled off to a convent. While there, at the age of 17, she was seduced by a Spanish army officer. In time, a marriage was arranged between the then 20-year-old Manuela and a middle-aged but wealthy English businessman, James Thorne. Her new husband, however, soon all but abandoned his young bride, leaving Manuela to pursue her passion for the emerg-ing revolutionary cause. By the time she met Bolívar, Manuela had already received the Peruvian "Dame of the Order of the Sun" for her efforts at spying in the independence movement. Bolívar had found his soul mate.

THE ODD COUPLE

The Liberator was not the only one doing liberation work for the patriot cause in South America—far from it. Indeed, the list is long and illustrious, and includes such notables as Mariano Moreno, José Artigas, Manuel Belgrano, Bernardo O'Higgins, and Manuela Pavon Unánue, among others. Yet standing above all of these men, and perhaps second in sig-nificance only to Simón Bolívar, is José de San Martín, the "Protector" and savior of the South. Today throughout the continent, and particularly in Argentina, it is Martín, not Bolívar, who is revered for his fight for the people's freedom and independence.

Though born in Argentina (in 1778), San Martín spent much of his early life in Spain, even serving there in the Spanish army. Returning to Buenos Aires in 1812, Martín, however, was quick to take up the cause for liberation, estab-lishing himself as a highly successful military leader.

In 1816, the "Protector" conceived one of the most dar-ing military actions in history. With 5,000 men, he crossed the Andes, through passes 12,000 feet (3,657.6 m) high, to descend upon surprised royalists at Chacabuco in February 1817. Though the undertaking had been planned for years, the

Although José de San Martín, a revolutionary and military hero much like Bolívar himself, announced the liberation of Peru in 1821, he had some trouble defeating the remaining royalist forces in the country. Martín turned to Bolívar for help (*above*) in ridding what was left of the Spanish military in Peru.

crossing was as perilous as any Bolívar experienced in traversing the northern Cordillera. "The rocky mountainsides rise from the river almost perpendicularly several hundred feet, with the narrow path of shelf having been made by scooping out or excavating the rock almost on the edge of the precipice. The path is from one to two feet [0.6 m] in width, just sufficient for the mule to pass. Looking up, the mountaintop is in the clouds. The precipice below is a look of horror. You look down a gulf of five hundred feet, at the bottom of which rolls the furious Mendoza River."[6]

Having established himself in Chile, in July 1821, Martín moved on to Lima, Peru, where he declared the country's independence on July 28. Yet, 15,000 royalist troops remained secure in the highlands, in and around Cuzco. A year later, out of pure frustration, Martín headed to Guayaquil, to confer with Simón Bolívar as to how they might cooperate in finally crushing all royalist resistance in South America.

Their meetings took place over a two-day period, on July 26 and 27, 1822. The two leaders conferred in private, behind closed doors—no one else was present. Virtually all later accounts, however, indicate that the two men, while prepared to exchange niceties, did not get along. "José de San Martín was a personality in complete contrast to the Liberator," wrote Robert Harvey. "His successes were accompanied by a selflessness and devotion to duty, the counterpart of the frenzied histrionics, the fevered and sometimes murderous determination exhibited by Bolívar."[7]

Martín wanted Bolívar's help in the final conquest of Peru. He would need a large contingency of Colombian troops for the effort. This was not something the glory-seeking Bolívar was willing to do. In truth, unless the Liberator could garner the entire honor for himself, he was reluctant to supply needed aid. In the end, in the effort to defeat the Spanish once and for all, there was no room for two supreme commanders. Martín, in a magnanimous gesture, would leave the effort to Bolívar. The Protector withdrew, exiting Lima for Chile in September. Soon after, he retired to France, where he died in 1850.

FINAL BATTLES

Following the fateful meeting of Bolívar and Martín, over 6,000 Colombian troops, led by Sucre, reached Peru in early 1823. In September, Bolívar followed. By May of 1824, the Liberator was ready to embark on his most risky campaign ever. He would march 9,000 men into the mountains, to the plain of Cerro de Pasco, at 12,400 feet (3,779.5 m). In June, if all went well, he would fight the royalists based in Cuzco.

The mountain climbing was arduous. One English general, a longtime veteran in Europe, described it as the most difficult military operation he had ever undertaken.[8] Of particular concern was the snow blindness many men were sure to experience. With it, "A pimple forms on the eyeball, and causes an itching prickling pain, as though needles were continually piercing it. The temporary loss of sight is occasioned by the

THE BOLIVIAN CONSTITUTION

In 1825, with the creation of the state of Bolivia (named after Simón Bolívar), the Liberator was invited to write the country's constitution—a distinct honor and one he took most seriously. Bolívar hoped that such a constitution would serve as a model for South American countries recently liberated. The constitution's most controversial feature called on the president to serve for life. Below are articles 76–78 of the Bolivian Constitution:

OF THE EXECUTIVE POWER

Article 76. The exercise of the Executive Power is vested in a president who serves for life, a vice-president, and three secretaries of state.

Article 77. The president of the Republic shall be named the first time by absolute plurality of the Legislative Body.

Article 78. To be named president of the Republic, one must:

Be an active citizen and native of Bolivia.

Be thirty years of age.

Have rendered important services to the Republic.

Have known talents in the administration of the state.

Never have been convicted of a criminal offense, however slight.

impossibility of opening the eyelids for a single moment, the smallest ray of light being absolutely insupportable. The only relief is a poultice [medicated mass] of snow, but as that melts away the tortures return."[9]

Upon reaching Cerro de Pasco on August 2, 1824, Bolívar reviewed his troops. "'Soldiers,' he declared, 'you are going to finish the greatest task which heaven can charge to a man: to save a whole world from slavery. . . . Soldiers, Peru and the whole of America are waiting for you to deliver peace, the child of victory."[10]

The battle that ensued, on August 6, lasted less than an hour. During the encounter, not a shot was fired—carnage was being inflicted with sword and lance. "A hard riding band of Patriot cavalry charged right in with their twelve-foot lances—the longest lances in the Americas—a deadly innovation introduced by San Martín back in Argentine days."[11] When the battle of Junín was over, the dead and wounded lay in great heaps. The royalists lost six times as many soldiers as did the patriots.

On December 9, 1824, in the battle of Ayacucho to the south, Sucre, with over 5,000 troops, engaged the last of the royalist forces, under the Peruvian viceroy, La Serna, with 9,300 men. Sucre told his men, "Upon your efforts depends the fate of South America."[12]

It was a strange battle that, at 12,000 feet (3,657.6 m), decided the patriot cause once and for all. "At the sound of bugles, Royalists and Patriots executed movements almost touching each other. The two sides suspended fire at intervals, and various opposing officers advanced and conversed together."[13] Still, when it was over, 1,900 Spanish troops lay dead, with 700 wounded. The patriots lost 310 dead, and more than 600 were hurt. The last great battle in the liberation of South America had concluded in a decisive republican victory.

BOLIVIA (UPPER PERU)

Late in1824, Sucre, the victorious young patriot general, made his way to Cuzco. From there, in early 1825, he moved on to

General Antonio José de Sucre, one of Bolívar's most trusted lieutenants, defeated Spanish forces in Ecuador—the only country that stood between Bolívar and Peru. Sucre later led more than 5,000 troops to victory in the Battle of Ayachucho (*above*), a win that would expel the remaining Spanish forces out of Peru.

La Paz, 325 miles (523 km) to the southeast. The ancient Inca city rests at 12,500 feet (3,810 m), in a bowl surrounded by high peaks. La Paz had, since its founding in 1548, developed into a thriving trade center on the route from Potosí to Lima.

Here, on February 9, Sucre decreed that delegates should be selected from the five provinces of Upper Peru and sent to a general assembly to decide the future of the region. They were given three choices: join with Argentina, become part of Peru, or go it alone as an independent nation. They immediately chose to become a free and separate country.

In April, Bolívar set out from Lima for Cuzco. Everywhere the Liberator went he was greeted as such. "Traditionally this sort of welcome was designed to placate conquerors or figures of authority and stave off punishment and pillage; this time the people were undoubtedly expressing genuine relief, welcoming a conqueror who exacted no vengeance."[14] Upon arrival in Cuzco on June 25, Bolívar issued a far-reaching decree. All forced labor was to be banned, and all employment was to be freely and fairly agreed to. Slavery, in other words, was to be a thing of the past. Furthermore, all communal land was to be divided among landless Indian peasants. To such peasants, Bolívar now became a godlike figure, an Inca chief reincarnate.

Initially, Bolívar had been annoyed with Sucre's proclamation of independence for Upper Peru, but he soon acquiesced. On August 19, 1825, Sucre accepted the Upper Peruvian Congress's decision to call the new independent state Bolivia, after the Liberator. Bolivar was overwhelmed by the honor but refused to assume the new country's leadership. Sucre became Bolivia's first president.

Bolívar was, however, invited to write Bolivia's first constitution. He eagerly accepted the challenge, hoping that what was produced would serve as a model for the rest of a free South America.

The new constitution's most striking feature was the provision whereby the powerful president would serve for life.

The president would also have the right to choose his successor. "This Bolívar regarded as 'the most sublime inspiration of republican ideas,' the president being 'the sun which, fixed in its orbit, imparts life to the universe'. . . . Thus 'elections would be avoided, which are the greatest scourge of republics and produce only anarchy.'"[15]

While Bolívar always favored a strong executive, his presidency for life, supposedly a compromise between legislative dominance and monarchy, represented a profound move toward authoritarianism and away from democracy. Seven years earlier, in Angostura, Bolívar had declared: "The continuation of authority in the same individual has frequently meant the end of democratic governments. Repeated elections are essential in proper systems of government."[16]

Bolívar, in the years ahead, would find his new constitution a tough sell in the countries he had freed. It would not, however, be the only "reality check" awaiting the Liberator.

8

Colombia Undone

The Spanish royalists, stubborn beyond all reason, held out in pockets against patriot forces until January of 1826. In one desperate case, General José Ramón Rodil, governor of Callao, remained holed up in the port city with 2,500 soldiers and 3,800 civilians. The inhabitants were soon reduced to eating rats, dogs, cats, and even their pack animals. Over 2,000 soldiers died, in many cases of scurvy and typhus. It was a senseless act that nonetheless earned Rodil the gratitude of his distant king, Ferdinand VII, who awarded his foolish bravado with an appointment as captain general of Cuba.

It had taken half a century, but the Western Hemisphere wars for independence were finally won. Beginning in 1775, with the battles of Lexington and Concord against British colonial domination in North America, to the victories of Bolívar and Sucre in 1825 over Spanish rule, freedom from European reign had been achieved. Spain would retain control of two Caribbean islands, Cuba and Puerto Rico, until the century's end, but they were small prizes in what was once the world's largest empire.

In leading the charge for independence, Bolívar had demonstrated unparalleled courage and stamina. Of the 696 battles fought to free Venezuela, Colombia, Ecuador, Peru, Bolivia, and Panama (a department of Colombia), the Liberator directly participated in almost 300. "The marches of his army exceeded in the aggregate those of Alexander to India and of Hannibal through Africa, Spain, and France to Italy, as well as of Jenghis [Genghis] and Kublai Khan and Tamerlane across Asia."[1] Many times over, the hard-riding, saddle-worn Liberator had earned his nickname, *Culo de Hierro* ("Iron Buttocks").

In the summer of 1826, Bolívar's Congress of Panama, which was a bold attempt at bringing together the newly independent Latin American countries to solve mutual problems, opened. It was, by the Liberator's account, a failure from the start. Only four states were represented: Mexico, Central America, Colombia, and Peru. Argentina and Chile refused to attend. Notably, the United States was not invited. Bolívar feared the expansionist tendencies of the "Colossus of the North," as well as believed that the differences between North Americans and South Americans were too great. "They are foreigners to us, if only because they are heterogeneous in character,"[2] Bolívar wrote. In addition, given the commercial and economic might of the United States, Bolívar was eager to avoid angering British interests.

Though a disappointment in Bolívar's eyes, the Congress of Panama did approve five basic principles of collaboration. The delegates pledged to accept: international arbitration in disputes between states, neutrality and coexistence among members, the Monroe Doctrine, recognition of the national sovereignty of member states, and the abolition of slavery. The last agreement was ahead of its time. Undoubtedly, had the United States sent delegates, they would have opposed the provision.

The Congress of Panama, in spite of its limited achievements, did create a precedent for future regional congresses. Establishment of the Organization of American States (OAS), in 1948, is testimony to its far-reaching goals.

VENEZUELAN BREAKAWAY

It is not surprising, with victory over the Spanish now achieved, that disintegrating forces quickly manifested themselves, something Bolívar had long feared and predicted. Ironically, it would be in Venezuela, the Liberator's home, where rebellion against united republican rule would appear strongest.

In truth, Gran Colombia arose out of an attempt to combine two very different states and peoples. Venezuela was a lawless, largely nonwhite tropical land ruled by caudillos (warlords) such as José Antonio Páez, Juan Bautista Arismendi, José Francisco Bermúdez, Santiago Mariño, and Rafael Urdaneta. New Granada, in turn, was overwhelmingly white, with a significant, prosperous middle class. It was ruled by the legalistic and scheming Santander, with a strong Congress to back him up. According to historian John Lynch, "The great distances separating Venezuela, Cundinamarca [Colombia] and Quito, the mountain ranges, the poor communications, the heterogeneous mass of the population, *pardos* of Venezuela, *mestizos* of New Granada, Indians of Ecuador, all made it impossible to unite greater Colombia or to infuse it with 'national character and national feelings.'"[3]

Santander, nominally in charge of all three regions, soon developed strong disagreements with Páez. In one notable incident, Santander ordered Páez to Bogotá to face charges of press-ganging thousands of men into military service. In response, Páez wrote to Bolívar, imploring him to take charge, to make himself a Napoléon of South America. The Liberator rejected the suggestion, fearing it would ruin his reputation. Nonetheless, Bolívar's fear of anarchy caused him

The differing opinions on how to govern Gran Colombia caused the relationship between Bolívar and his vice-president, Francisco de Paula Santander (*above*), to degenerate from friendship into hatred. Santander was determined to discredit and undermine the aging Bolívar.

once again to reiterate his strong support of authoritarian (and elitist) rule:

> I am convinced to the very marrow of my bones that America can only be ruled by an able despotism. . . . We are the vile

offspring of the predatory Spaniards who came to America to bleed her white and to breed with their victims. Later the illegitimate offspring of these unions joined with the offspring of slaves transported from Africa. With such racial mixture and such a moral record, can we afford to place laws above leaders and principles above men?[4]

On January 1, 1827, Bolívar, now in Puerto Cabello, announced an agreement with the rebellious Páez. He would pardon the caudillo's men and grant Páez complete civilian and military authority in Venezuela, thus (in Bolívar's eyes) avoiding civil war. In turn, Páez consented to recognize Bolívar as supreme leader and president of Gran Colombia. In a ceremony in Caracas, the Liberator gave Páez a jewel-encrusted sword, whereupon the grateful recipient wept with gratitude.

While Bolívar had, for now, defused civil war, his actions infuriated Santander. In the vice president's view, Bolívar, having set out to put down an insurrection by Páez, wound up accepting it. Bolívar, Santander contended, had all but recognized Venezuelan independence. He was presiding over the destruction of his own creation, Gran Colombia, in order to save Venezuela from bloodshed. The die was cast. From this moment on, Santander and Bolívar would become bitter, intractable enemies.

SANTANDER'S BETRAYAL

Bolívar remained in Caracas for the first half of 1827, reorganizing various branches of the administration, in particular the treasury. On July 5, the anniversary of the first Venezuelan declaration of independence, the Liberator left for Bogotá, via Cartagena, on board a British warship. He was accompanied by Sir Alexander Cockburn, the British minister. The Liberator would never return to the city of his birth—indeed, he would never again set foot in Venezuela. Bolívar was aging, and it showed. "He was not yet forty-four, but looked older, his eyes sunk in his colorless, cadaverous face, his cheeks hollow. He was still capable of sudden bursts of immense energy and irresistible charm, but often fell into lassitude and irritability."[5]

Arriving in Bogotá, he embraced Santander, though by now their relationship had gone from camaraderie, to rivalry, to outright hatred. The Liberator immediately summoned Manuela, who was living in Quito. "Your goodness and graces reanimate the ice of my years," Bolívar wrote to the woman he cherished. "Your love animates a life which is expiring. I cannot be without you, I cannot deprive myself voluntarily of you, Manuela. . . . Come, come, come."[6]

A contemporary described Bolívar's lover thus: "She was always visible . . . her arms were bare; she took no trouble to hide them. . . . She talked little; she smoked gracefully. . . . During the day she would appear dressed as an officer. In the evening she was transformed. She certainly wore rouge. Her hair was artistically combed. She was very animated. She was happy, sometimes using quite risqué language. Her graciousness and generosity were limitless."[7] For Bolívar, Manuela had become indispensable.

The Liberator was in need of soothing—his empire was revolting and breaking apart on numerous fronts. There was news of an abortive rebellion in Bolivia. In October, fresh fighting had broken out in Venezuela. In Cartagena, Admiral Padilla led an uprising, though it was quickly quelled. In Peru, a revolt of the Third Division was followed by a change in government, whereby the Peruvians aborted a version of the Bolivian constitution.

In response to the alarming news from afar, the Congress in Bogotá was quick to express complete confidence in Bolívar, immediately ratifying all of his Venezuelan measures of January 1, 1827. The Congress also granted the Liberator "extraordinary powers," giving him the right to, in effect, take the government into his own hands.

Although Bolívar had acquired immense powers, there was much his enemies, in particular Santander, could do to thwart the Liberator's efforts in maintaining control. As Bolívar's long-sought Great Convention, to be held in Ocaña to ratify a new constitution, approached, his vice president set about scheming to undermine the president's position. Santander traveled the land, securing the election of delegates committed to a weak central government, both for New Granada and Venezuela. A confrontation (not only between two powerful, determined leaders but between two ideologies) seemed unavoidable.

SIMÓN BOLÍVAR AND GEORGE WASHINGTON

Much has been written comparing Simón Bolívar and George Washington. While their lives and achievements were similar in some respects, they differed in many ways. Bolívar was reluctant to embrace American governmental forms, particularly that of the executive. George Washington was, of course, the first elected president. Nonetheless, when in 1826 the United States sent Bolívar a medallion (and other mementos) of Washington that symbolized a connection between the two great freedom fighters, the Liberator was overcome with gratitude. Writing to Joseph Lafayette, on Mach 20, 1826, Bolívar said, in part:

> Words cannot express how greatly my heart cherishes so glorious an assembly of thoughts and objects. Washington's family honors me in a manner far exceeding my remotest hopes, as a reward from Washington, given by the hand of Lafayette, is the ultimate in human compensations. . . . My embarrassment is equaled only by the infinite sense of gratitude with which I tender Your excellency the respect and veneration due the Nestor of human freedom.

Richard W. Slatta & Jane Lucas De Grummond. *Simón Bolívar's Quest for Glory*. 6.

OCAÑA FAILURE

When the Ocaña convention began its deliberations on April 9, 1828, 68 deputies were in attendance. They had been chosen from two main factions. One, with the support of Bolívar, sought a constitution strong in executive power and in the preservation of Gran Colombia. Under the leadership of Santander, another set of delegates clamored for federalism, though exactly what regions were to be federated was unclear. A third, smaller caucus demanded outright independence for Venezuela, New Granada, and Quito (Ecuador). In other words, they sought the breakup of Gran Colombia.

Bolívar did not attend the convention, preferring, instead, to hole up in Bucaramanga, a provincial town two days' ride from Ocaña. Here he would remain to monitor events and answer any summons that might be received.

Santander was only too pleased that Bolívar, his archrival, was not present at Ocaña. In a frank admission of the Liberator's continuing charisma and ability to sway all around him, Santander conceded: "Such is his influence and the secret force of his mind that upon an infinite number of occasions, even, I, full of vengeance, have encountered him and merely seeing and hearing him, have been disarmed and have gone away filled with admiration. Nobody can oppose General Bolívar face to face; and unhappy he that attempts it."[8]

Be that as it may, the Liberator did send a message to the convention, sketching a somber picture of Gran Colombia. As Bolívar saw it: "Colombia, which managed to spring to life, lies lifeless. . . . Colombia, which breathed an atmosphere of honor and virtue in the face of oppressive forces, now gasps for air as if it were unaware of its national dishonor. Colombia, which one thought only of painful sacrifices and distinguished service, now thinks only of its rights, not its duties. The nation would have perished if some remnant of public spirit had not driven it to cry out for remedy and drawn it up short of the edge of the grave."[9]

Bolívar waited and waited for a call to the convention, staying in Bucaramanga for close to 70 days. The invitation never came. The Liberator spent most of his time reading, playing cards, horseback riding, jogging, and, rather unusual for him, attending church services. The last activity was seen by some detractors as an insincere attempt to curry favor with the Catholic Church. It was noted that Bolívar was once seen reading a book during Mass and that he never crossed himself.

On June 11, 1828, the convention at Ocaña dissolved in acrimony, with nothing accomplished. Two days earlier, Bolívar had left for Bogotá, having been asked by its leaders to assume "supreme authority," lest anarchy and Gran Colombian disintegration prevail. The Liberator was greeted as a savior. In one of his first official acts, Bolívar eliminated the office of vice president and appointed Santander as minister to the United States to get rid of him. Dictatorship, it now seemed, was the only force that could preserve Gran Colombia.

THE LOVABLE FOOL

On July 13, in full military dress in Bogotá's Cathedral Plaza, the Liberator took the oath of office before Congress as absolute dictator. Bolívar was given full powers in every sphere of government "to reorganize every branch of government in the way he considered best to care for internal evils, conserve the union, and establish foreign credit."[10] The dictator moved into San Carlos Palace, with its ample corridors, fireplaces, and bathtubs. Manuela Sáenz took a house nearby.

Bolívar's mistress, ever her unconventional self, had by now gained a decidedly scandalous reputation. Every night she held balls and dances. "She appeared at her gatherings in gowns of the latest French and British styles, with daring décolleté and glittering jewelry. Her behavior at these gatherings was often shocking to many; certainly her conduct and her tongue were both free-wheeling."[11]

On July 24, to celebrate Bolívar's birthday, Manuela arranged a huge party. The Liberator did not attend, though

Manuela Saenz, Bolívar's mistress, threw wild parties and constantly shocked people with her language, dress, and demeanor. Although Bolívar referred to her as his "lovable fool," she was smart and quite aware of the dangers surrounding her lover. She urged Bolívar not to disregard his enemies or their actions against him.

his entire cabinet, now called the council, did. Manuela had her black female slave, Jonotás, put together an old sack of sawdust, adorned with black eyes and long mustachios. On the sack was a sign labeled "Santander, killed for treason." "Soldiers dragged it by a rope and propped it against a wall, a leading Catholic dean gave it last rites, then Colonel Richard Crofston of the British legion gave the command to fire."[12] The sawdust sack that was the former vice president was blown to smithereens.

To Bolívar, his "lovable fool" had definitely gone too far. Although what Manuela did was to some extent a private, not public, affair, the Liberator was genuinely shocked. He gave Manuela orders to avoid such publicity in the future. He threatened to banish his mistress from the city and threatened to send her back to Quito.

Manuela, not surprisingly, would acquiesce to none of this. Having stood up to everyone and anyone, her lover would be no exception. Manuela warned Bolívar that if he was not firm and decisive with his enemies, particularly Santander, he would bring about his own demise. If they so much as lifted their heads, she advised sternly, they should be killed.

Perhaps ominously, Manuela was on to something. Bolívar issued a peremptory order to have Santander leave the country for the United States, and to do so by September 5. Both Manuela and Bolívar feared that plotting to overthrow the regime could well be under way. The so-called Philological Society of Bogotá, supposedly a literary discussion group, was in reality a center of conspiracy aimed at the Bolívarian dictatorship. Made up of mostly young, liberal, professional men, with a few military officers to boot, it was here that plots were hatched—including those of assassination. Bolívar, as Manuela had warned, was undoubtedly in grave danger.

9

The Last
Dictatorship

At close to midnight, on September 25, 1828, the worst suspicions of both Manuela and Bolívar were confirmed, though the Liberator, but a few hours earlier, made light of any coup possibility. "There may be ten so far as you are concerned, to judge by the way you deal with warnings," Manuela reproached Bolívar, as he took a bath in the palace of San Carlos. "Don't worry, nothing will happen," the Liberator retorted. Bolívar's mistress later recalled, "He [Bolívar] made me read to him, then went to bed and slept deeply, with no other precautions than his sword and pistols handy; no other guard than the usual, no warning to the officer in charge, content with the assurances of the Chief of Staff that he would answer for everything."[1]

The conspirators were 26 in number—10 civilians under Augustín Horment and 16 privates commanded by Lieutenant Colonel Carujo. After gathering earlier in the evening at the house of Luis Vargas Tejada, the would-be attackers divided into three groups. One, headed by Horment and Carujo, left to strike the presidential palace and kill Bolívar. A second contingency planned to assault the barracks of the Vargas Battalion to free General José Padilla from jail. A third group would storm the grenadiers at their headquarters. "Towards midnight two of his [Bolívar's] dogs barked, and I heard some strange noises,"[2] Manuela noted later. "I woke up the Liberator, and the first thing he did was to take up his sword and a pistol and try to open the door."[3]

Swiftly, the two guard dogs were killed, as were three sentries. The plotters then thrust their way forward, where they assaulted Ibarra, Bolívar's personal bodyguard, badly injuring him. William Ferguson, a young British legionnaire, was stabbed to death defending the door to Bolívar's bedroom.

Manuela, who had been sleeping with the Liberator, quickly helped him dress, placing his small feet into her slippers. Bolívar then tried to open the door, his purpose to confront the intruders directly. Manuela, however, pulled her lover back, urging him instead to escape out their first-story window. When the sidewalk cleared of pedestrians, Bolívar jumped. An instant later, Manuela rushed to the hallway. The assassins, grabbing her, demanded where Bolívar had gone. "I said he was in the council chamber, which was the first thing that came into my head," Manuela was later to explain. "They searched the outer room carefully, went into the bedroom, and seeing the open window, exclaimed, 'He has escaped. He has saved himself.'"[4]

In response to her obvious deception, Manuela was severely beaten, so much so that she would subsequently spend 12 days in bed. But Bolívar had indeed escaped. With the aid of his chief retainer, José Palacio, the two made their way down to the San Agustín River, where they took refuge beneath the arches of the Carmen Bridge. After three anxious, weary hours, Bolívar ordered Palacio to search for their allies. Finally,

Bolívar came out of hiding and—numb, drenched, and covered with mud—rode into the main square, where he was greeted enthusiastically. The Liberator responded, "'Do you want to kill me with joy when I am on the point of dying with grief?'"[5] Bolívar's cause for distress was (in his eyes) obvious; he had been humiliated, his glory perhaps tarnished forever.

REPRISALS

Ever faithful, Manuela was on hand to lift Bolívar's spirits. Though wounded in the head and a hand, his mistress had quickly made it to the plaza in search of her lover. As Bolívar embraced her, he cried, "Manuela! My Manuela, the liberatress of the Liberator!"[6]

Within hours of the assassination attempt, General Urdaneta had hundreds of suspects rounded up and in handcuffs. "A gallows was erected in front of the cathedral, and a few soldiers were hung at once. For four days, depositions were taken."[7] Bolívar, feeling ill and distraught, wanted to declare an amnesty for all. But Urdaneta and Bolívar's supporters would have none of it. A trial, with a court of eight, was set up. Verdicts were not long in coming.

"The first executions began before a large crowd. Vendors sold cakes, bread, fruit, and blue-gold-red cockades of the Republic. The drums sounded, and Colonel Ramón Guerrera was marched in, hands bound in front grasping a huge crucifix. Next came big black Admiral Padilla and four others. . . . Guerrera died after a brief macabre dance. But Padilla's bull neck did not break. He burst his thongs and tore at the rope. Soldiers rushed up and fired point-blank into his body."[8] The hangings continued for weeks.

Santander was arrested on September 30. His part in the coup has never been fully determined, with the general belief that, while sympathetic to the cause, the ex–vice president played no direct role in planning or executing the rebellion of September 25. Though initially condemned to death, Bolívar,

In deep contrast to the way he entered Caracas for a triumphant victory parade in 1829 (*above*), Bolívar came out from hiding under a Bolivian bridge after surviving an assassination attempt. Weak and dispirited, he was willing to pardon the conspirators and assassins, but his supporters refused and insisted on trial and punishment.

in a most magnanimous gesture, commuted his sentence to perpetual exile. (Santander would later return as president of an independent Colombia.)

Bolívar, though having escaped assassination (for the third time), was now seriously ill—broken physically and morally. Clearly, he was suffering from debilitating tuberculosis. Though only 46, to more than a few who saw him, he appeared a man in his sixties. The French minister, writing after a short visit, noted:

"When we addressed our first words to him about his health, he replied, waving his skinny arms, 'Ah, it is not the laws of nature which have put me in this state, but the burdens that weigh upon my heart. My fellow countrymen, who could not kill me with knives, are now trying to assassinate me morally with their ingratitude and calumnies [slanders]. When I stop existing, the demagogues will devour each other like wolves, and the edifice I built with superhuman efforts will sink into the mud of revolution.'"[9]

Unfortunately, an accurate omen, indeed.

CITIZEN-IN-ARMS

South American countries that had struggled so hard for their independence from colonial rule now fought for independence from each other's domination. In particular, a major border dispute had erupted, whereby Colombia and Peru claimed Ecuadorian territory. Clearly, Gran Colombia was on the verge of collapse. Bolívar, it would seem, had no sway over the territories he had liberated. Sick and ever more disillusioned, the Liberator nonetheless undertook yet one more mission to the South to launch a campaign against Peruvian forces. He would remain in the region through most of 1829.

It was at this time that rumors began to circulate, particularly in Gran Colombia, that Bolívar was contemplating the reactionary step of establishing a monarchy, in the hopes of creating both social stability and preserving his political legacy. Of course, liberals, particularly in Colombia, were outraged.

In truth, Bolívar had little enthusiasm for such a scheme, even declaring in a humorous way that "no foreign prince would wish to rule so anarchic a land [as in South America], or one so unable to sustain a lavish court."[10] Bolívar certainly saw no role for himself as the monarch. As O'Leary reported, "It never was meant that General Bolívar should be crowned, nor were his services to be required by laying him upon the shelf. It was intended to have him elected chief magistrate, *ad vitam* under the popular title of Liberator. After his death the foreign prince was to succeed."[11]

Early in 1830, Bolívar returned to Bogotá pale, emaciated, in almost total collapse both in body and spirit, yet having successfully put down rebellion in Peru. He told Manuela, who came out to greet him, that, "I seem an old man of sixty!"[12]

On January 20, a new Congress met to adopt a loose federal constitution, the type Bolívar had always feared as being too weak. In April, the Liberator resigned his dictatorship. "Do as you will with the presidency, which I respectfully deliver into your hands," he told congressional delegates. "Henceforth, I am but a citizen-in-arms, ready to defend my country and obey her government. My public duties are forever ended. I formally and solemnly deliver to you the supreme authority conferred upon me by the express wish of the nation."[13]

Bolívar's dream of a united northern South America lay in ruins. Gran Colombia was no more, finally being divided into the three completely independent states of Colombia, Ecuador, and Venezuela. Liberals and federalists would have no part of a centralized government and a strong chief executive. Bolívar, the supreme general who could defeat all advisories on the battlefield, was unable to deliver unity in peace. "Unlike George Washington, his North American counterpart, Bolívar could not make the transition from soldier to statesman. No longer needing his military leadership and finding his dictatorship odious, even one-time friends turned against him."[14]

Bolívar accepted his fate, leaving Bogotá for the coast on May 8, 1830. "My glory! My glory! Why do they take it from me?"[15] were his departing words.

SIMÓN BOLÍVAR AS ECOLOGIST

Even nearly 200 years ago, there were individuals well aware of the need to conserve precious natural resources, particularly forest products. Simón Bolívar was such a person, as his statement on "Measures for the Protection and Wise Use of the Nation's Forest Resources," written in Guayaquil, Ecuador, on July 31, 1829, shows. As liberator president of the Republic of Colombia, Bolívar declared:

> First, that the Forests of Colombia, those owned publicly as well as privately, represent an enormous treasure in wood suitable for all types of construction as well as dyes, quinine, and other useful substances for medicine and the arts.
>
> Second, that throughout the region we are experiencing excessive harvesting of wood, dyes, quinine, and other substances, especially in forests belonging to the state, with disastrous consequences.
>
> Third, that to avoid these, it is necessary to establish regulation for the effective protection of public and private property against violations of every kind, having seen the reports compiled for the government on this matter and heard the report of the Council of State,
> I hereby decree

The Liberator then went on to present 10 articles restricting the use of forests, so that their products could be rationed and preserved for future generations. Clearly, Bolívar was an ecological leader well ahead of his time.

JOURNEY'S END

Within a few days, Bolívar reached the Magdalena River and by May 25 was at the outskirts of Cartagena. His plan was to sail for Europe and exile. Some historians claim that Bolívar saw his voluntary removal from South America's disintegrating political scene as temporary, that the Liberator foresaw a time when he would be recalled once more to lead a united Gran Colombia. It was not to be.

Either for lack of ships or poor accommodations, Bolívar did not immediately embark. For several grueling months, he remained waiting in the hot, humid, unhealthy climate of the Colombian coast. By early December, the Liberator was clearly dying. A French doctor, Alexandre Prospére Révérend, examined Bolívar and concluded that, among other aliments, he had pulmonary and meningeal tuberculosis. It was a grim prognosis.

Though his physical condition deteriorated daily, Bolívar's mind remained alert. On December 10, 1830, he issued a heart-rending proclamation to "the People of Colombia," which read, in part: "My enemies have played upon your credulity and destroyed what I hold most sacred—my reputation and my love of liberty. . . . If my death will help to end party strife and to promote national unity, I shall go to my grave in peace."[16]

Shortly thereafter, Bolívar penned his most famous and pessimistic line: "He who serves a revolution ploughs the sea."[17] It was a bitter observation from a nearly totally disheartened liberator.

Bolívar now drifted in and out of delirium. He told those at his bedside that he wished to be buried in his birthplace, the city of Caracas. In truth, at least while he lived, Bolívar was barred from ever again setting foot in Venezuela.

The Liberator's last days were uncomfortable and restless. He fought for breath as he was moved from bed to hammock and back again. "Let's go! Let's go!" were Bolivar's last words, spoken as if in a dream. "People in this land do not want me. Come boys! Take my luggage on board the frigate."[18]

Simón Bolívar, the liberator of six South American countries, died at midday on December 17, 1830. He was 47 years old. Bolívar's remains were taken to Santa Marta, where it was reported that "His body was embalmed, and laid in state. . . . His funeral took place on the 20th, among much love and gratitude."[19]

Manuela had been summoned to Bolívar's bedside but arrived a day too late. Utterly distraught, she supposedly attempted suicide by inviting a poisonous snakebite. Though his mistress would go on to outlive Bolivar by 26 years, dying in 1856 during a diphtheria epidemic in Paitá, Peru, they would not be happy years. Most were spent suffering the spite and hostility of Bolívar's enemies.

DEMAGOGUE TO DEMIGOD

On February 9, 1842, 12 years after Bolívar's death, José Antonio Páez, president of Venezuela, petitioned Congress to have the Liberator's remains returned to Caracas, an act that would fulfill Bolívar's deathbed wish. On hand to receive his ashes was Hipólita, his elderly black nurse. Of Bolívar, Páez wrote:

> Simon Bolívar belongs to the band of modern men whose equals are to be found only when we reach back to republican times of Greece and Rome. . . . In the midst of people who had no more tradition than the respect for an authority sanctioned by the acquiescence of three centuries of ignorance, superstition, and fanaticism, nor any political dogma but submission to an order of things supported by might and force, Bolívar succeeded in defying that power.[20]

Though the glorification, indeed, deifying, of Bolívar had begun, there were those who sought to debunk the hero-worship, to define the Liberator as a demagogue. They pointed to his wasted youth; his inexcusable betrayal of his mentor,

THE CULT OF BOLÍVAR

When Simón Bolívar's remains were returned to Venezuela in 1842, escorted by the warships of powerful nations, José Antonio Páez, the country's president, declared, "The prosperity of Venezuela was the first thought of Bolívar, the first motive of his heroic deeds; we have omitted nothing we could possibly do in honoring his memory. It is not the triumph of Bolívar that we celebrate: it is also the triumph of Venezuela."*

Thus, what has become known as the Cult of Bolívar was born, where there would be no shortage of those—historians, journalists, politicians, priests, and presidents—eager to promote an idealized Bolívar for their cause. As John Lynch observed, the cultists had a good story to tell. "A hero of pure Venezuelan lineage, after a tragic marriage and golden youth in Europe, assumes the leadership of national independence, provides the intellectual base of a continental revolution, and then the military and political talents to create a union of states and win international respect, all the time asserting his manhood as a glorious lover. There were many Bolívars here, with any of whom people could identify. Venezuelan nationalist, American hero, macho male, Bolívar conformed to the roles. . . . Bolívar was a model for the nation."**

Miranda; the tragic wars to the death; of his repeated failures in liberating Venezuela (with its resulting tremendous cost and suffering); the cold-blooded murder of hundreds of prisoners of war; and, perhaps most telling, his vanity, posturing, preening, and incessant quest for glory.

Of the last, glory, there is little doubt it was the guiding passion of the Liberator. "From the very beginning of his public life he wanted glory, believing that he had earned glory, and demanded that others recognize his glory," wrote historian John Lynch. "His concern for glory, his awareness of his own greatness, was not simply one aspect of his inner self; it defined

In December of 1998, many Venezuelans were surprised to discover that their country had been renamed "the Bolívarian Republic of Venezuela" by its new president, Hugo Chávez. "God is the supreme commander, followed by Bolívar, and then me,"[***] the unabashed self-proclaimed Bolívarian declared.

The cult of Bolívar has clearly been used by military dictators throughout Latin America to further their own causes. For some such leaders, he is a populist Bolívar, for others a socialist Bolívar. Both distort who Bolívar really was and what he stood for. Nonetheless, Simón Bolívar left an enormous legacy, one that in his quest for glory freed six countries from colonial domination and set them on a path, tortured and long as it has been, to independence and nationhood. As historians Richard W. Slatta and Jane Lucas De Grummond noted, "Bolívar's words and deeds serve as powerful reminders that one determined individual, even one with serious flaws of character and temperament, can dramatically shape the course of human history."[****]

---

[*]John Lynch. *Simón Bolívar: A Life*. 300.

[**]Ibid. 301.

[***]Richard W. Slatta & Jane Lucas De Grummond. *Simón Bolívar's Quest for Glory*. 308.

[****]Ibid. 310.

his character and inspired his actions. It seemed to be the wellspring of his life."[21]

Yet, glory, at least in Bolívar's eyes, was an honorable achievement, a compound of honor, recognition, and fame. It was something won in battle and then noted with pride. For Bolívar, glory need not be, and often was not, accompanied by power.

Today, Simón Bolívar is revered throughout Latin America. He is seen as having achieved unimaginable victory on the battlefield, while at the same time providing the revolution's indispensable intellectual leadership, generating its

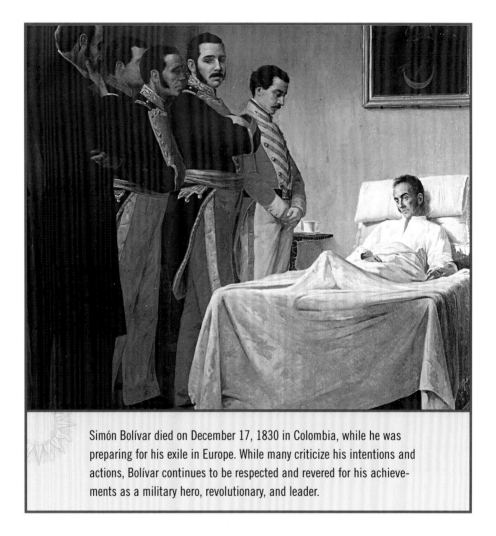

Simón Bolívar died on December 17, 1830 in Colombia, while he was preparing for his exile in Europe. While many criticize his intentions and actions, Bolívar continues to be respected and revered for his achievements as a military hero, revolutionary, and leader.

prime source of ideas and arguments. Yet, above all, Bolívar is remembered as a man of action, one capable of demonstrating incredible physical endurance, durability, and willpower. "This [willpower] sustained him through twenty years of unremitting struggle, driving him tens of thousands of miles along primitive roads and tracks, and across plains and mountains in one of the longest of colonial wars. . . . This was heroism on a grand scale."[22]

Of Bolívar, it has been said that he stands head and shoulders above any other figure Latin America has produced. Clearly, the Liberator demonstrates that, even with notable flaws in personality, one man can dramatically shape the course of history. "Does his achievement matter, in view of the suffering the continent has endured since his day?" asked Robert Harvey, rhetorically. "The answer must be an unequivocal 'yes.' It matters that Latin America was freed from a decaying parasitic empire. It is not the Liberator's account that after its release the continent has taken nearly two centuries to stand on its feet."[23]

Indeed, though "doomed to death though fated not to die,"[24] Simón Bolívar has defied history; his transformation from demagogue to demigod is today all but complete.

Chronology

1783   Born Simón José Bolívar, in Caracas, Venezuela, on July 24.

1799   Bolívar goes to Spain to study.

1802   Bolívar marries María Teresa de Toro, in Madrid, Spain, on May 26.

1803   Maria dies in Caracas. Bolívar pledges never to marry again.

1805   Bolívar, having returned to Europe, makes his vow on Monte Sacro to fight for Venezuelan independence.

1808   Napoléon I conquers Spain and deposes Ferdinand VII.

1811   Venezuela declares independence from Spain on July 5.

1812   Massive earthquake strikes Venezuela on March 26, killing 20,000 people. First Republic falls.

1783
Born Simón José Bolívar, in Caracas, Venezuela, on July 24

1811
Venezuela declares independence from Spain on July 5

1783   1813

1802
Bolívar marries María Teresa de Toro, in Madrid, Spain, on May 26

1813
On May 14, Bolívar begins "Admirable Campaign." On June 18, he declares "war to the death," and on August 6, he is named "Liberator"

1813   On May 14, Bolívar begins "Admirable Campaign."
        On June 18, he declares "war to the death," and on
        August 6, he is named "Liberator."

1814   Second Venezuela Republic collapses.

1815   Bolívar arrives in Jamaica; writes his famous "letter."

1816   Bolívar returns to Venezuela with expeditionary
        force.

1819   Bolívar elected president of the Third Republic of
        Venezuela. He crosses the Andes to defeat the Spanish
        at Boyacá.

1821   Battle of Carabobo ends Spanish rule in northern
        South America.

1822   Quito (Ecuador) falls after battle of Bomboná.
        Bolívar meets with San Martín at Guayaquil on July 26.

1819
Bolívar elected
president of the
Third Republic of
Venezuela. He crosses
the Andes to defeat
the Spanish at Boyacá

1822
Quito (Ecuador)
falls after battle of
Bomboná. Bolívar
meets with San
Martín at Guayaquil
on July 26

1830
Bolívar dies of
tuberculosis on
December 17

1819   1830

1821
Battle of Carabobo ends
Spanish rule in northern
South America

1824
Spanish defeated at
battle of Ayacucho on
December 12, ending
Spanish resistance in
South America

1824   Spanish defeated at battle of Ayacucho on December 12, ending Spanish resistance in South America.

1826   Bolívar calls Congress of Panama.

1828   Bolívar survives assassination attempt on September 25.

1830   Gran Colombia dissolves. Bolívar dies of tuberculosis on December 17.

Notes

Chapter One

1 John Lynch, *Simón Bolívar: A Life*. New Haven, Conn.: Yale University Press, 2006, 26.
2 Ibid.
3 Robert Harvey, *Liberators: Latin America's Struggle for Independence*. Woodstock, N.Y.: The Overlook Press, 2000, 62.
4 Ibid. 69.
5 Richard W. Slatta & Jane Lucas De Grummond, *Simon Bolivar's Quest for Glory*. College Station: Texas A&M University Press, 2003, 23.
6 Quoted in Benjamin Keen, ed., *Latin American Civilization: History & Society, 1492 to the Present*. Boulder, Colo.: Westview Press, 1991, 472.
7 Ibid. 216.
8 Ibid. 219.
9 Robert Harvey, *Liberators*. 73.
10 Ibid. 74.
11 John Lynch, *Simón Bolívar*. 48.
12 Ibid.

Chapter Two

1 Robert Harvey, *Liberators*. 20.
2 Ibid. 79.
3 Ibid. 80.
4 David Bushnell, *Simón Bolívar: Liberation and Disappointment*. New York: Pearson Longman, 2004, 31.
5 Robert Harvey, *Liberators*. 81.
6 Ibid.
7 John Lynch, *Simón Bolívar*. 2.
8 Robert Harvey, *Liberators*. 82–83.
9 Ibid.
10 Ibid. 84.
11 Ibid. 86.
12 Ibid. 87.
13 Ibid.

Chapter Three

1 Robert Harvey, *Liberators*. 99.
2 John Lynch, *Simón Bolívar*. 66.

3 Frederick H. Fornoff, *El Libertador: Writings of Simón Bolívar*. New York: Oxford University Press, 2003, 3.
4 Robert Harvey, *Liberators*. 103.
5 John Lynch, *Simón Bolívar*. 72.
6 Ibid. 73.
7 Ibid.
8 Robert Harvey, *Liberators*. 112.
9 Ibid.
10 Richard W. Slatta & Jane Lucas De Grummond, *Simón Bolivar's Quest for Glory*. 81.
11 Ibid.
12 Ibid. 82.
13 John Lynch, *Simón Bolívar*. 75.
14 Robert Harvey, *Liberators*. 118.
15 Ibid. 120.
16 Ibid.
17 Ibid. 122.
18 Ibid. 123.

Chapter Four

1 Robert Harvey, *Liberators*. 129–130.
2 John Lynch, *Simón Bolívar*. 86–87.
3 Ibid. 111–112.
4 Robert Harvey, *Liberators*. 137.
5 Ibid. 138.
6 Frederick H. Fornoff, *El Libertador*. 25.
7 Ibid. 26.
8 David Bushnell, *Simón Bolívar*. 69.
9 Richard W. Slatta & Jane Lucas De Grummond, *Simón Bolivar's Quest for Glory*. 130.
10 Robert Harvey, *Liberators*. 143.
11 David Bushnell, *Simon Bolivar*. 83.
12 Robert Harvey, *Liberators*. 145.
13 Ibid. 151.
14 John Lynch, *Simón Bolívar*. 107.

Chapter Five

1 John Lynch, *Simón Bolívar*. 203.
2 Richard W. Slatta & Jane Lucas De Grummond, *Simón Bolivar's Quest for Glory*. 147.

3 Ibid. 170.
4 Robert Harvey, *Liberators*. 165.
5 Richard W. Slatta & Jane Lucas De Grummond, *Simón Bolívar's Quest for Glory*. 174–175.
6 Alfred Hasbrouck, *Foreign Legionaries in the Liberation of Spanish South America*. New York: Octagon Books, 1969, 36.
7 Ibid. 38.
8 Frederick H. Fornoff, *El Libertador*. 45.
9 Robert Harvey, *Liberators*. 174.
10 Marion Lansing, *Liberators and Heroes of South America*. Boston: L.C. Page & Company Publishers, 1940, 192.
11 Ibid. 192–193.
12 Richard W. Slatta & Jane Lucas De Grummond, *Simón Bolívar's Quest for Glory*. 188.
13 Irene Nicholson, *The Liberators: A Study of Independence Movements in Spanish America*. New York: Frederick A. Praeger, Publishers, 1968, 190.
14 Richard W. Slatta & Jane Lucas De Grummond, *Simón Bolívar's Quest for Glory*. 190.
15 David Bushnell, *Simón Bolívar*. 109.
16 Robert Harvey, *Liberators*. 182.
17 Ibid. 183.

Chapter Six
1 Daniel A. del Rio, *Simón Bolívar*. Clinton, Mass.: The Colonial Press Inc., 1965, 72.
2 John Lynch, *Simón Bolívar*. 135.
3 Marion Lansing, *Liberators and Heroes of South America*. 198.
4 Ibid. 199.
5 Ibid.
6 John Lynch, *Simón Bolívar*. 140.
7 Marion Lansing, *Liberators and Heroes of South America*. 201.
8 Robert Harvey, *Liberators*. 191.
9 Daniel A. del Rio, *Simón Bolívar*. 80.

10 John Lynch, *Simón Bolívar*. 143.
11 Ibid. 145.
12 Ibid. 146.

Chapter Seven
1 Robert Harvey, *Liberators*. 194.
2 Ibid.
3 Carleton Beals, *Eagles of the Andes: South American Struggles for Independence*. New York: Chilton Books, 1963, 224.
4 Ibid. 225.
5 Ibid.
6 Marion Lansing, *Liberators and Heroes of South America*. 81–82.
7 Robert Harvey, *Liberators*. 199.
8 Lauran Paine, *Bolívar the Liberator*. New York: Roy Publishers, 1970, 374.
9 Robert Harvey, *Liberators*. 220.
10 Ibid. 221.
11 Carleton Beals, *Eagles of the Andes*. 224.
12 Lauran Paine, *Bolívar the Liberator*. 378–379.
13 Richard W. Slatta & Jane Lucas De Grummond, *Simón Bolívar's Quest for Glory*. 253.
14 Robert Harvey, *Liberators*. 253.
15 John Lynch, *Simón Bolívar*. 202.
16 Ibid.

Chapter Eight
1 Richard W. Slatta & Jane Lucas De Grummond, *Simón Bolívar's Quest for Glory*. 258.
2 David Bushnell, *Simón Bolívar*. 151.
3 John Lynch, *Simón Bolívar*. 219–220.
4 Ibid. 217–18.
5 Robert Harvey, *Liberators*. 256.
6 Ibid.
7 Ibid.
8 Marion Lansing, *Liberators and Heroes of South America*. 239.
9 David Bushnell, *Simón Bolívar*. 181

10 Carleton Beals, *Eagles of the Andes: South American Struggles for Independence*. 298.

11 Ibid. 297.

12 Ibid. 299.

Chapter Nine

1 Salvador De Madariaga, *Bolívar*. New York: Pellegrini & Cudahy, 1952, 570.

2 Ibid. 570–571.

3 Robert Harvey, *Liberators*. 263.

4 Ibid.

5 Salvador De Madariaga, *Bolívar*. 572.

6 Carleton Beals, *Eagles of the Andes*. 304.

7 Ibid.

8 Ibid.

9 Robert Harvey, *Liberators*. 264.

10 Ibid. 267.

11 Ibid. 266.

12 Ibid. 269.

13 Richard W. Slatta & Jane Lucas De Grummond, *Simón Bolívar's Quest for Glory*. 288.

14 Ibid. 289.

15 Robert Harvey, *Liberators*. 291.

16 Richard W. Slatta & Jane Lucas De Grummond, *Simón Bolívar's Quest for Glory*. 291.

17 Marshall C. Eakin, *The History of Latin America: Collision of Cultures*. New York: Palgrave Macmillan, 2007, 189.

18 John Lynch, *Simón Bolívar*. 278.

19 Richard W. Slatta & Jane Lucas De Grummond, *Simón Bolívar's Quest for Glory*. 292.

20 Robert Harvey, *Liberators*. 291.

21 John Lynch, *Simón Bolívar*. 293.

22 Ibid. 297.

22 Robert Harvey, *Liberators*. 278.

24 John Lynch, *Simón Bolívar*. 302.

Bibliography

Books

Adams, Jerome R. *Latin American Heroes: Liberators and Patriots from 1500 to the Present*. New York: Ballantine Books, 1991.

Beals, Carleton. *Eagles of the Andes: South American Struggles for Independence*. New York: Chilton Books, 1963.

Boyd, Bill. *Bolívar: Liberator of a Continent*. New York: S.P.I. Books, 1998.

Burkholder, Mark A., and David S. Chandler. *From Impotence to Authority: The Spanish Crown and the American Audiences, 1687–1808*. Columbia: University of Missouri Press, 1977.

Bushnell, David. *Simón Bolívar: Liberation and Disappointment*. New York: Pearson Longman, 2004.

Del Rio, Daniel A. *Simón Bolívar*. Clinton, Mass.: The Colonial Press, Inc., 1965.

Dominguez, Jorge I. *Insurrection of Loyalty: The Breakdown of the Spanish-American Empire*. Cambridge, Mass.: Harvard University Press, 1980.

Eakin, Marshall C. *The History of Latin America: Collisions of Cultures*. New York: Palgrave Macmillan, 2007.

Fornoff, Frederick H. *El Libertador: Writings of Simón Bolívar*. New York: Oxford University Press, Inc., 2003.

Harvey, Robert. *Liberators: Latin America's Struggle for Independence 1810–1830*. Woodstock & New York: The Overlook Press, 2000.

Hasbrouck, Alfred. *Foreign Legionaries in the Liberation of Spanish South America*. New York: Octagon Books, 1969.

Johnson, John J. *Simón Bolívar and Spanish American Independence 1783–1830*. Princeton, N.J.: D. Van Nostrand Company, Inc., 1968.

Keen, Benjamin, ed. *Latin American Civilization: History & Society, 1492 to the Present*. Boulder, Colo.: Westview Press, 1991.

Langley, Lester D. *The Americas in the Age of Revolution: 1750–1850*. New Haven, Conn.: Yale University Press, 1996.

Lansing, Marion. *Liberators and Heroes of South America*. Boston: L.C. Page & Company Publishers, 1940.

Lynch, John. *San Martin: Argentine Soldier, American Hero*. New Haven, Conn.: Yale University Press, 2009.

Lynch, John. *Simón Bolívar: A Life*. New Haven, Conn.: Yale University Press, 2006.

Lynch, John. *The Spanish-American Revolutions, 1808–1826*. New York: W.W. Norton & Co., 1986.

Madariaga, Salvador de. *Bolívar*. New York: Pellegrini & Cudahy, 1952.

Marquez, Gabriel Garcia. *The General and his Labyrinth*. London: Penguin Books, Ltd., 1991.

Masur, Gerhand. *Simón Bolívar*. Albuquerque: University of New Mexico Press, 1948.

Nicholson, Irene. *The Liberators: A Study of Independence Movements in Spanish America*. New York: Frederick A. Praeger, 1968.

Olson, James S. *Historical Dictionary of the Spanish Empire, 1402–1975*. New York: Greenwood Press, 1992.

Paine, Lauran. *Bolívar the Liberator*. New York: Roy Publishers, 1970.

Petrie, Loraine F. *Simón Bolívar: "El Libertador."* New York: Best Books, 1924.

Rock, David. *Argentina, 1516–1982: From Spanish Colonization to the Falklands War*. Berkeley: University of California Press, 1985.

Rodríguez O., Jamie E. *The Independence of Spanish America*. Cambridge: Cambridge University Press, 1998.

Slatta, Richard W., and Jane Lucas De Grummond. *Simon Bolivar's Quest for Glory*. College Station: Texas A&M University Press, 2003.

Web Sites

The Battle of Boyacá
http://www.btinternet.com/~alan.catherine/wargames/boyacoob.htm

El Libertador
http://www.geocities.com/Athens/Acropolis/7609/eng/bio.html?200912

Independence in Latin America
http://www.fsmitha.com/h3/h39-la.html

José De San Martin—The Knight of the Andes
http://www.geocities.com/TimeSquare/1848/martin.html?20097

José De San Martin's Home Page
http://www.pachami.com/English/ressanmE.htm

Latin American Independence
*http://encarta.msn.com/encyclopedia_761588450/Latin_American_
Independence.html*

Latin American Independence: Politics & Government
*http://historicaltextarchive.com/sections.
php?op=viewarticle&artid=307*

Llaneros—Cowboys of Colombia and Venezuela
http://gosouthamerica.about.com/od/venartandculture/a/llaneros.htm

Seize The Night: Napoleon I
http://www.carpenoctem.tv/military/napoleon.html

Seize The Night: Simón Bolívar
http://www.carpenoctem.tv/military/bolivar.html

South American Wars of Independence
*http://au.encarta.msn.com/text_781534780__1/South_American_
Wars_of_Independence.html*

Wars of South American Independence: Battle of Boyacá
http://militaryhistory.about.com/od/battleswars1800s/p/boyaca.htm

Films

Simón Bolívar (The Hispanic and Latin American Heritage Video
Collection), Schlessinger Video, 1999.

Further Reading

Books

De Varona, Frank. *Simón Bolívar: Latin American Liberator*. New York: Houghton Miffin Harcourt (HMH), 1993.

Goodnough, David. *Simón Bolívar: South American Liberator*. Springfield: Enslow Publishers, Inc., 1998.

Greene, Carol. *Simón Bolívar: South American Liberator*. New York: Childrens Press, 1889.

Slatta, Richard W. *Gauchos and the Vanishing Frontier*. Lincoln: University of Nebraska Press, 1992.

Wepman, Dennis. *Simón Bolívar (World Leaders Past & Present)*. New York: Chambers, 1985.

Web Sites

History of Simón Bolívar
http://www.bolivarmo.com/history.htm

Latin America
http://www.trincoll.edu/classes/hist300/group3/latin.htm

Latin American Chronology
http://www.ilstu.edu/class/hist127/chron.html

Latin American History
http://latinamericanhistory.about.com/od/latinamericaindependence/a/independence.htm

Latin American Wars of Independence
http://www.answers.com/topic/latin-american-wars-of-independence

Simón Bolívar
http://www.embavenez-us.org/kids.venezuela/simon.bolivar.htm

Viceroy
http://www.answers.com/topic/viceroy

Picture Credits

Index

About the Author

Ronald A. Reis has written young-adult biographies of Eugenie Clark, Jonas Salk, Mickey Mantle, Ted Williams, Lou Gehrig, Sitting Bull, and Buffalo Bill, as well as books on the Dust Bowl, the Empire State Building, the New York City subway system, African Americans and the Civil War, and the World Trade Organization. He lives in Los Angeles and can be reached at ronelect@aol.com.